THE WAR
AFTER THE WAR

Significant Issues Series
Timely books presenting current CSIS research and analysis of interest to the academic,
    business, government, and policy communities.
Managing editor: Roberta L. Howard

For four decades, the **Center for Strategic and International Studies (CSIS)** has been
    dedicated to providing world leaders with strategic insights on—and policy solutions
    to—current and emerging global issues.

   CSIS is led by John J. Hamre, formerly deputy secretary of defense, who has
been president and CEO since April 2000. It is guided by a board of trustees chaired
by former senator Sam Nunn and consisting of prominent individuals from both the
public and private sectors.

   The CSIS staff of 190 researchers and support staff focus primarily on three
subject areas. First, CSIS addresses the full spectrum of new challenges to national
and international security. Second, it maintains resident experts on all of the world's
major geographical regions. Third, it is committed to helping to develop new
methods of governance for the global age; to this end, CSIS has programs on
technology and public policy, international trade and finance, and energy.

   Headquartered in Washington, D.C., CSIS is private, bipartisan, and tax-exempt.
CSIS does not take specific policy positions; accordingly, all views expressed herein
should be understood to be solely those of the author.

The CSIS Press
Center for Strategic and International Studies
    1800 K Street, N.W., Washington, D.C. 20006
    Telephone: (202) 887-0200 Fax: (202) 775-3199
    E-mail: books@csis.org Web: www.csis.org

THE WAR AFTER THE WAR

Strategic Lessons of Iraq and Afghanistan

Anthony H. Cordesman

THE CSIS PRESS

Center for Strategic
and International Studies
Washington, D.C.

Significant Issues Series, Volume 26, Number 4
© 2004 by Center for Strategic and International Studies
Washington, D.C. 20006
Printed on recycled paper in the United States of America
Cover design by Robert L. Wiser
Cover photograph: U.S. Troops Continue to Stabilize Baghdad @ Cheryl Diaz Meyer/
    Dallas Morning News/Corbis

08 07 06 05 04   5 4 3 2 1

ISSN 0736-7136
ISBN 0-89206-450-1

Library of Congress Cataloging-in-Publication Data
Cordesman, Anthony H.
        The war after the war : strategic lessons of Iraq and Afghanistan / Anthony H.
    Cordesman.
            p. cm. — (Significant issues series ; v. 26, no. 4)
Includes bibliographical references.
            ISBN 0-89206-450-1
1. Iraq War, 2003. 2. Iraq War, 2003—Diplomatic history. 3. War on Terrorism, 2001-
        4. United States—Military policy. 5. National security—United States.
I. Title. II. Series.
DS79.76.C677 2004
327.730567'09'0511—dc22
                                                    2004011306

CONTENTS

PREFACE

The United States may still be able to achieve some form of victory in Iraq if it persists, commits the necessary resources, and accepts the real-world limits on what it can do. No one can predict how the combination of nation building, low-intensity combat, and Iraqis' efforts to recreate their nation will play out over the short term, but the United States has ten tools it can use to achieve the best strategic outcomes. Since May 2003, the United States has shown it is adaptable and it is making some use of all of these tools:

- Accept the fact that Iraq's interests and solutions will differ from those of the United States.
- Shift the U.S.-led information campaigns and efforts to win hearts and minds of Iraqis to Iraqi-led endeavors.
- Stay the military course and, concurrently, develop Iraqi security and armed forces as quickly as possible.
- Transfer political and administrative power as rapidly as possible to Iraqis; transfer should be on Iraqi terms.
- Maintain a high level of aid, yet allow Iraq to reform its economy on its own terms.
- Sustain efforts to win forgiveness of Iraqi debts and reparations.
- Ensure energy investment and development on Iraqi terms.
- Plan now for at least a five-year period of continued U.S. engagement after full Iraqi sovereignty.

- Engage Iraq's neighbors.
- Engage the United Nations and the international community.

THE OTHER WARS

Iraq is the most important near-term challenge, but it is not the only one. The United States must look beyond Iraq and deal with its other "wars" and security interests. No U.S. strategy that focuses on Iraq alone is an adequate approach to the future. Almost without sensing the drift, America found itself involved in four separate and simultaneous conflicts, some of which may require active U.S. intervention for another decade or more. Each of the other conflicts also requires shifts in U.S. policy.

The war in Afghanistan. Nation building is in crisis in Afghanistan, but at less cost and largely without high-profile media examination. The United States cannot deal with the Afghan conflict by simply transferring security and nation-building responsibilities to NATO or international control. If it tries, the result will almost certainly be a resurgence of Taliban or Islamic extremism in some form, continued warlordism, and a drug-based economy that inevitably spills into the Middle East and Central Asia. The necessary effort does not need to be on the scale of the effort in Iraq, but the United States must provide substantial resources over a period of some five to ten more years. It will almost certainly mean spending some $5 to $10 billion more than the United States currently anticipates over the next five years.

The war on terrorism. The United States by itself cannot afford to engage every terrorist movement, and it risks alienating and radicalizing peoples and movements in nations throughout the Islamic world if it does so. It needs to create local partnerships with key nations like Saudi Arabia and Indonesia. It needs to focus systematically on the considerable differences among the Sufi, Salafi, neo-Wahhabi, and Shi`a movements and deal with each separately on the terms best tailored to defeating violence and extremism in each case. The United States must also look beyond words like "democracy" and remember that it is a republic, not a democracy, that protects the individual over the majority and that preserves the rights of all through limitations on the power of the federal government and the system of checks and balances. Before the United States acts in the war on terrorism, it must remember that revolution—not evolution—brings misery to the nations where it takes place and violence and hostility to the United States.

The Arab-Israeli conflict. Here the United States does not have good options; it cannot abandon Israel or sacrifice its security. Therefore the United States should plan for the Israeli-Palestinian war to be a major strategic liability for the next five to ten years. There is no way out of this predicament other than a continuing and high-visibility U.S. effort to create a peace, regardless of how many times new initiatives fail. The United States will not win Arab hearts and minds by doing this, but it can increase Arab tolerance. Moreover, Israel's strategic interests—even more than U.S. strategic interests—ultimately lie in a successful peace. Israel's social structure and economy cannot be sustained through constant low-level war. The United States will never be at existential risk because of the proliferation of weapons of mass destruction in the Middle East; in a matter of years Israel could be.

STRATEGY AND STRATEGIC LESSONS

If the United States is to succeed in these wars and in similar conflicts that are likely to shape much of the twenty-first century, it must learn from its successes and its mistakes in Iraq and Afghanistan. Strategic engagement requires an objective—not an ideological—assessment of the problems that demand action and of the size and cost of the effort necessary to achieve decisive grand strategic results. Neither a strategy based on capabilities nor a strategy based on theoretical sizing contingencies is meaningful when real-world conflicts and well-defined contingencies require a strategy and force plan that deal with country-by-country realities.

Internationalism. There is no alternative to internationalism. At times the United States might disagree with the United Nations (UN) or some U.S. allies, but U.S. strategy must be based on seeking consensus wherever possible, on compromise when necessary, and on coalitions that underpin virtually every action the United States takes.

Coalitions. Great as U.S. power is, it cannot substitute for coalitions and the effective use of international organizations, regional organizations, and nongovernmental organizations (NGOs). To lead, the United States must also learn to follow. The United States must never subordinate its vital national interests to the interests of other countries, but this will rarely be an issue. In practice, the U.S. challenge is to subordinate U.S. arrogance to the end of achieving true partnerships, and to shape diplomacy to create lasting coalitions of the truly willing instead of coalitions of the pressured or intimidated.

Nation building. Armed nation building is a challenge only the United States is currently equipped to meet. Although U.S. allies, the UN, and NGOs can help with many aspects of security and nation-building operations, they often cannot operate on the scale required to deal with nation building in the midst of serious low-intensity combat.

Deterrence and containment. Deterrence and containment are more complex now than they were during the Cold War, but they are still critical tools and they, too, depend on formal and informal alliances.

War and diplomacy. War must be an extension of diplomacy by other means, but diplomacy must be an extension of war by other means as well. U.S. security strategy must be based on the understanding that diplomacy, peace negotiations, and arms control are also an extension of—and substitute for—war by other means. It is easy for a superpower to threaten force but far harder to use it; and bluffs get called. Fighting should be a last resort, and other means must strive to limit the number of fights.

Stabilization. Military victory in asymmetric warfare can be virtually meaningless without successful nation building at the political, economic, and security levels. Stabilization operations—also called Phase IV operations—are far more challenging than the defeat of conventional military forces and can be conducted best if the United States is prepared to act immediately after the defeat of conventional enemy forces. In both Afghanistan and Iraq, the United States wasted critical days, weeks, and months in security efforts that allowed opposition movements to regroup and then re-engage. U.S. actions created a power vacuum instead of exploiting one. The United States was unprepared for nation building and for the escalation of resistance once the enemy was defeated conventionally.

Manpower skills.   Force transformation cannot be dominated by technology; manpower skills, not technology, should be dominant. Low-intensity-combat missions, economic aid, civil-military relations, security, and information campaigns require skilled military manpower as well as new forms of civil expertise in other departments. Human intelligence (HUMINT) can still be more important than technical collection; local experience and language skills are critical; and the astute use of aid dollars can be more important than marksmanship.

Force numbers.   Neither the addition of troops and weapons nor their diminution through the use of technology will solve America's skilled-manpower problems. The missions that are emerging require skilled and well-trained troops with area expertise, linguists in far greater numbers, and specialists in civic action and nation building as well as guerrilla warfare.

Limits of technology.   Technology-based force transformation and the revolution in military affairs are tools with severe and sometimes crippling limits. The ability to provide intelligence, surveillance, and reconnaissance (IS&R) coverage of the world is of immense value. IS&R coverage does not, however, provide the ability to understand the world; deal with complex political issues; fight effectively in the face of terrorism, many forms of low-intensity conflict, and asymmetric warfare; terminate conflicts; make peace; and protect nation building. In practice, the United States may need to make far more effective use of legacy systems and evolutionary improvements in weapons and technology to support the "human-centric" forms of military action that require extensive HUMINT and area skills, high levels of training and experience, and effective leadership that not only defeat the enemy in battle but also win the peace.

Jointness.   Jointness cannot be limited to restructuring the U.S. military; the problem it addresses is larger than that. Jointness must occur within the entire executive branch, for civil-military jointness as well as for military-military jointness. A national security affairs adviser whose job is simply advisory is a failed national security affairs adviser; effective leadership is required to force coordination on the U.S. national security process. Unresolved conflicts between leaders like Secretary of State Colin L. Powell, and Secretary of Defense Donald H. Rumsfeld, the exclusion of other cabinet members from key tasks, insufficient review of military planning, and great power residing with small elements within given departments have weakened U.S. efforts and needlessly alienated our allies. The creation of a large and highly ideological foreign policy staff in the vice president's office is a further anomaly in the interagency process. The U.S. interagency process cannot function with such loosely defined roles, a lack of formal checks and balances, and a national security affairs adviser who does not have the power and responsibility to force interagency cooperation. Jointness must go far beyond the military; it must apply to all national security operations.

Complexity. Policy, analysis, and intelligence must accept the truth that the world is complex, deal with complexity honestly and objectively, and seek evolution while opposing revolution. The United States cannot afford to rush into—or stay in—any conflict on ideological grounds, just as it cannot afford to avoid any necessary commitment because of idealism. The United States must stop oversimplifying, sloganizing, mirror imaging, and prescribing democratization as the solution or even a first priority for every country. The United States must handle security threats quietly and objectively, country by country and movement by movement. U.S. decisionmakers should be informed pragmatists.

The United States must understand that successful reform in economic growth, limiting population increase, and furthering human rights may often be more important in the near term than progress toward elections. In fact, democracy, if it is defined as elections, is purposeless—even actively destructive—unless accompanied by viable political parties, political leaders capable of moving toward moderation and economic development, and enough of a national consensus to allow different ethnic, ideological, and religious factions to function in a stable pluralistic structure. The United States must act with the understanding that other societies and cultures can often find very different solutions to political, social, and economic modernization.

Organizational reform. Stabilization, armed nation building, and peacemaking require a new approach to organizing U.S. government efforts. The integration of the U.S. Agency for International Development (USAID) into the U.S. Department of State has compounded the problems of U.S. aid efforts. Because the United States had previously transferred many generic aid projects to the World Bank and International Monetary Fund, USAID had no staff prepared, sized, and trained to deal with nation building on the scale imposed by Iraq; neither was USAID able to formulate and administer the massive aid program required. Contractors were overburdened with large-scale contracts because the government found them easiest to grant and administer despite the contractors' lack of operational experience in a command economy and a high-threat environment. U.S. government and contractor staff—often with limited experience—had to be suddenly recruited for three- to twelve-month tours of duty, tours too short to ensure continuity in such missions. Denial of the importance and scale of the mission beforehand does not prevent the need for aid programs when reality intervenes.

New capabilities are required within the National Security Council, the Department of State, and the Department of Defense for security and nation-building missions. It does not matter whether these are called post-conflict, Phase IV, stabilization, or reconstruction missions. The United States must be as well prepared to win a peace as it is prepared to win a war. It must have the interagency tools in place to provide security after the termination of a conflict and to support nation building by creating viable political systems, economic stability and growth, effective military and security forces, a system of public information, and a free press. This requires the National Security Council to have relevant expertise, the State Department to have organizational and operational capabilities, the Department of Defense to have the appropriate military capabilities, and other agencies to be ready to support the efforts.

The United States must never repeat its most serious mistakes in Iraq and Afghanistan. From the start, the United States must make security and nation building fundamental parts of the planning and execution of military operations directed at foreign governments. A clear operational plan must be prepared before military operations begin; costs and risks should be fully assessed; and Congress should be consulted as it is consulted before the commencement of military operations. Security and nation-building missions must proceed in tandem with combat operations, and without a pause that creates a power vacuum. The United States must from the start ensure that the necessary resources for nation building are present.

Military cooperation.   U.S. military strategy must give military advisory efforts and interoperability the same priority as jointness. The United States needs to rethink its arms sales and security assistance policies and work with other arms sellers to reduce the volume of sales. It also needs to work with regional powers toward making the arms they do need effective and sustainable, creating local security arrangements and improving interoperability for both deterrence and war fighting. The United States needs to recast its security assistance programs to help nations fight terrorism and extremism more effectively, in ways that do not abuse human rights or delay necessary political, social, and economic reforms.

Public relations.   The United States needs to organize for effective information campaigns while it seeks to create regional and allied campaigns that will influence Arab and Islamic worlds. The United States needs to revitalize its information efforts in a focused and effective way so that while working in foreign countries it can take advantage of tools like satellite broadcasting and the Internet. The United States, however, can never be an Arab or Islamic country. It needs to work with its friends and allies in the region to create information campaigns that reject Islamic radicalism, violence, and terrorism and support reform. The United States should not try to speak for the Arabs or for Islam; it should help them speak for themselves.

Investment and funding.   The U.S. private sector and foreign direct investment should be integrated into U.S. security strategy and efforts to achieve evolutionary reform. When it deals with hostile or radical states, the United States has tended to emphasize sanctions over trade and economic contact, and it assigns too low a priority to helping the

U.S. private sector invest in friendly states. It is time for a zero-based review of how the U.S. government should encourage private sector activity in the Middle East.

Intelligence reform.   Current methods of intelligence collection and analysis cannot guarantee adequate preparation for stabilization operations, support low-intensity combat properly, or support nation building properly. The United States needs to fundamentally reassess its approach to intelligence in order to support adequate planning for the combat termination, security, and nation-building phases of asymmetric warfare and peacemaking operations. It is equally important that adequate tactical intelligence support—HUMINT support, area expertise, and linguistic skills—be available from the beginning of combat operations to the end of security and nation-building operations. Technology can be a powerful tool, but technology is an aid—not a substitute—for human skills and talents.

New approaches are needed at the tactical and field levels to create effective teams for operations and intelligence. Tactical intelligence must contribute to team effort along with counterinsurgency operations, the political and economic phases of nation building, security, and military advisory teams. It is particularly critical that both intelligence and operations directly integrate combat activities with civil-military relations efforts, U.S. military police and security efforts, economic aid used in direct support of low-intensity combat and security operations, the training and integration of local security forces into the HUMINT effort, and the creation of effective information campaigns.

Current methods of intelligence collection and analysis and current methods of arms control and inspection cannot guarantee an adequate understanding of the risks posed by proliferation. The United States needs to fundamentally reassess the problems of intelligence on proliferation and the lessons Iraq provides regarding arms control. Media coverage and outside analysis of intelligence failures in Iraq have focused far too much on the politics of the situation or have implied that intelligence failed because it was improperly managed and reviewed. Long-standing problems in Central Intelligence Agency (CIA) management of its counterproliferation efforts and CIA institutional biases affected almost all intelligence community reporting and analysis on the subject.

Defense resources.   The United States has agonizing decisions to make about defense resources. The current Future Years Defense Program (FYDP) makes it obvious that the United States cannot provide funding for both its planned force levels and its force improvement plans. Everyone with any experience stopped believing long ago in estimated procurement costs. The United States faces years of unanticipated conflicts, many involving armed peacemaking and nation building, and it must rethink deterrence in terms of proliferation. This is not a matter of billions of dollars; it is a matter of several percentage points of the U.S. gross national product (GNP).

New commitments.   Limit new strategic adventures where possible. The United States needs to avoid additional military commitments and conflicts unless they truly serve vital strategic interests. It already faces serious strategic overstretch, and nothing could be more dangerous than assuming that existing problems can be solved by adding new undertakings such as Syria or Iran. Emphasis should be placed on deterrence, containment, and diplomacy to avoid additional military commitments; it means a new emphasis on international action and allies to find substitutes for U.S. forces.

One final reality—the image of a quick and decisive victory is almost always a false one, but it is still the image many Americans want and expect. A thousand or more dead in Iraq is hardly Vietnam, but it must be justified and explained honestly—not in ephemeral slogans. The budget increases and supplements of the past few years are also likely to be the rule and not the exception. The United States may well have to spend another 1 percent of its GNP on sustained combat and international intervention overseas. Yet no U.S. politician is willing to admit this.

The United States faces hard political choices, choices that will demand exceptional leadership and courage in both the election year of 2004 and in the decades to come. They require bipartisanship of a kind that has faded since the Cold War, and neither neoconservative nor neoliberal ideology can help. Moreover, think tanks and the media— and politicians and military planners as well—must move beyond sound bites and simple solutions. This year—2004—is going to be a very tough year; it is also going to be a very tough decade.

Source: Central Intelligence Agency.

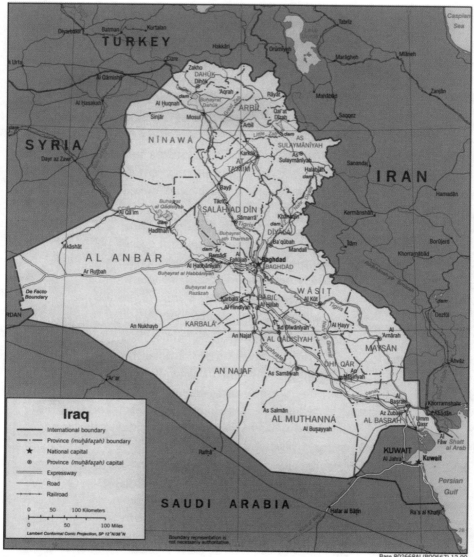

Source: Central Intelligence Agency.

CHAPTER ONE

REALITIES OF HISTORY

It is tempting to focus on America's short-term problems in Iraq, particularly during an election year. The fact is, however, that the United States is involved in four major conflicts in the Middle East, and U.S. actions have more than a tactical meaning. The United States is fighting not only in Iraq but also in Afghanistan, in a broader war of terrorism, and by proxy in the Arab-Israeli conflict.

America's actions are shaping the future in both strategic and grand strategic terms, and the longer-term strategic context of the actions will ultimately determine the consequences for U.S. security policy and for the U.S. position in Iraq and in the greater Middle East. It is therefore critical to begin to focus on the strategic lessons that are emerging from the Iraq War, the U.S. engagement in Afghanistan, the war on terrorism, and the Arab-Israeli conflict.

As a preface to the analysis of these consequences, it is useful to remember George Santayana's statement, "Those who cannot remember the past are condemned to repeat it." Santayana's statement has always been troublesome because anyone who truly remembers history is all too well aware that history is always repeated, regardless of whether it is remembered. At the same time, Americans perpetually forget four basic lessons of history:

- History takes time; nothing moves half as quickly as Americans would like to assume.

- History is filled with uncertainty, and it cycles erratically. Few trends are consistent, particularly trends toward an idea of progress.

- History is complex. It does not lend itself to simple analyses, ideologies, and solutions; and it is filled with unintended consequences when policymakers attempt simplistic approaches.

- History can have tremendous momentum and be almost impossible to change.

Americans accept none of these points easily, particularly in Washington, a city in which every new administration seeks to restructure the world in four to eight years. Furthermore, most Americans are optimists, at least when they are in charge of the government and are actively seeking to influence events.

We expect too much too soon, and we usually minimize risk. We forget that life is filled with risk and uncertainty. When reality intervenes and reminds us of this historical reality, the optimism turns to pessimism with equal speed. We do not like discovering that risk is inevitable and that many trends and their consequences are beyond our control.

CHAPTER TWO

REALITIES OF IRAQ

Observers can debate the rationale for the war in Iraq, its timing, and the degree of international consensus. It is clear that there were major problems in the U.S. and British intelligence on proliferation. It is also clear that the United States was as badly prepared for nation building, the security mission, and low-intensity combat as it was well prepared to defeat Iraq's conventional forces and force the collapse of Saddam Hussein's regime. It can be argued that many of these failures—in nation building, the security mission, and low-intensity combat—have also extended the war in Afghanistan and led to the war's expansion into Pakistan.

The fact that the United States still has a great deal to learn about the strategic and military realities of the twenty-first century does not mean it can avoid dealing with them. The wars in Iraq, Afghanistan, and against terrorism are wars in which a refusal to have fought them would almost certainly have at best deferred the challenges involved, and would probably have made them far worse. Containment could not have dealt with Saddam Hussein, the Taliban, or Al Qaeda; it would have merely allowed the situations to fester and the groups to grow stronger.

The United States cannot afford any further illusions regarding the challenges it faces in Iraq and what it can and cannot hope to accomplish. In fact, Iraq is a test case of how to combine all of the region's challenges into one country.

DEMOGRAPHICS AND JOBS

Iraq faces a long-term population explosion. Despite sanctions, war, and mass graves, the U.S. Census Bureau estimates that Iraq's population has leaped from 5.1 million in 1950, and 13.2 million in 1980—the beginning of the Iran-Iraq War—to some 25 million in 2004. The fertility rate (per woman) is 4.9 and the rate of natural increase is 2.9 percent. Conservative Census Bureau estimates indicate the population will rise to 30 million in 2010, 37 million in 2020, and 44 million in 2030.

Jobs are a critical problem, which will grow with time. Some 530,000 young men and women now enter the workforce each year, and unemployment is at 50–60 percent. This number will rise to more than 800,000 per year by 2025. Approximately 40 percent of the population has been affected by the educational problems that began during the Iran-Iraq War, problems that became steadily graver after 1990 as a result of the Gulf War and sanctions.

LEADERSHIP

The United States and its allies have at best won a limited window of tolerance from most Iraqis. Until at least the establishment of an elected government, which the United States does not plan to see until early 2006, it must be prepared to deal with continued challenges from former regime loyalists, other hostile Sunnis, and foreign and domestic Islamic extremists. Many Iraqis actively oppose the coalition, and the United States faces a situation so unstable that the Shi`a majority could become hostile or the country could drift toward civil conflict.

During Saddam's tyranny, the current Iraqi leadership was denied needed experience. Iraq's political problems have been made worse by nearly three decades of dictatorship, nearly continuous war and sanctions, a failed command economy, and ruthless political purges. Roughly 70 percent of the population has never known any political leader other than Saddam and no political organization other than the Ba`th Party. No rival political leaders or parties could develop in Iraq, and leaders returned from exile unable to win the people's trust.

This situation is further complicated by the fact the coalition has been able to establish neither an interim government that has had broad popular support nor leaders with a strong following among the

Iraqi people. Polls of popular opinion show the members of the Interim Governing Council have little collective or individual support, and initially sovereignty will have to be transferred to a government with limited legitimacy and leaders with little popular support.

The Iraqi people have a national consciousness but are deeply divided. They have no real political experience and live with deep ethnic divisions. Although Saddam's government did not take a census recently, Iraqis are probably 60 percent Shi`a Muslim Arabs, 20 percent Sunni Muslim Arabs, 15 percent Kurds, and 5 percent Turcoman and other groups. Sunni and Shi`a are further divided by tribe, between people with rural and urbanized ways of life, and in terms of how religious or secular individuals are. An ABC News poll conducted in February 2004 shows the differences in attitude between and within the main ethnic and sectarian groups:

Question	Sunni Arabs	Shi`a Arabs	Kurds
Was Iraq humiliated or liberated?			
Humiliated	66	37	11
Liberated	21	43	82
Was the invasion right or wrong?			
Right	24	51	87
Wrong	63	35	9
Should the coalition leave now?			
Yes	29	12	2
Are attacks on coalition forces acceptable or unacceptable?			
Acceptable	36	12	2
Unacceptable	57	85	96
Preferred political system:			
Democracy	35	40	70
Strong leader for life	35	23	6
Islamic state	15	26	8
Preferred political system after one year:			
Single strong leader	65	44	20
Democracy	14	24	60
Religious leaders	5	18	2
Preferred political system after five years:			
Single strong leader	49	32	16
Democracy	31	39	67
Religious leaders	6	7	2

Guilt by association affects Iraq's ability to draw on its people's talents and skills. The most experienced technocrats, managers, police officers, and military officers are all tarred by their association with the former regime.

In addition, Iraq has no history of an adequate structure of law for dealing with security, civil law, criminal law, and human rights. The coalition rapidly created a mix of more than 200,000 Iraqi security forces, but most have had little training and most of those trained have little experience. Coalition efforts to supply them with the equipment they need have encountered shortages, and because the security personnel are recruited locally they often either are not loyal or are unwilling to risk a confrontation with hostile elements. The court system is making progress and the legal code is being improved, but Iraq in the past never experienced a real rule of law; it will be years before a workable legal system is fully in place.

Information has been government dominated at every level. Iraqi people have no basis of trust in the media or in authority, and Iraqis have had to turn to sources outside their country for anything approaching the truth.

ECONOMY

The economy has long been a state-controlled kleptocracy favoring the minority in power and giving guns priority over butter. Few economies in the region have less real-world experience with global competition and the free market. (8).

Oil

The oil sector has been crippled by years of underfunding, lack of technology, state mismanagement, and overproduction of key reservoirs. Many pipelines and large centralized facilities are vulnerable to sabotage and terrorism.

Oil income is Iraq's only significant export income and funds practically all of the state budget, but it is grossly inadequate to meet current and future needs. Department of Energy estimates that oil-sector earnings in real dollars have gone from $58 billion in 1980 (in constant 2000

U.S. dollars) to a maximum of $12.3 billion in 2002. Earnings will probably be $9–$12 billion in 2003, a bit more than $15 billion in 2004, and $19 billion in 2005. Even with an expansion of petroleum exports to 6 million barrels per day (mbd), it is unlikely that real per capita oil income during the next decade can be more than half of what it was in 1980 in constant dollars.

Agriculture

The agricultural sector has been driven by inefficient state planning and subsidies that never resulted in more than half the productivity Iraq should have had and that produced crops with large portions of inedible output. Approximately 60 percent of Iraq's food has been imported, and farmers have no experience with financing their crops or marketing them on a competitive basis.

Infrastructure

Utilities and infrastructure have been crippled by underfunding that began in 1982–1984, cannibalization, and fragmented organization. Most systems favor urban and Sunni areas, and services such as water and sanitation are grossly inadequate in slums and in many Shi`a areas.

Investment

Foreign investment in Iraq has been illegal, and Iraq has no real banking system in the Western sense. Industrial employment has been dominated by some 200–250 state industries, of which roughly 48 have been critical employers. None is remotely competitive in global terms, and most cannot survive competition from imports. The former massive military industries no longer exist.

U.S. NATION BUILDING

It is unsurprising under these circumstances that postwar nation building in Iraq has proved to be an extraordinary challenge at the political, economic, demographic, social, ethnic, and religious levels. This challenge has been compounded because, after the fall of Saddam Hussein's regime, U.S. officials and contractors with virtually no experience working in Iraq or in transforming a command economy had to improvise almost every aspect of nation building in an environment of increasing low-intensity combat.

 Paying for Iraq's Reconstruction, the Congressional Budget Office report of January 2004, estimates that $50–$100 billion will be needed for nation building during 2004–2007. Although this total does not begin to cover the full cost of creating a new economy and meeting the backlog of human needs, it may still sharply underestimate the scale of the funding required, even if war and sabotage do not add further major burdens. Total reconstruction expenses and Iraqi government budgets could range from $94 to $160 billion during this period, but oil revenues are estimated to range from $44 to $89 billion and seem likely to total well under $70 billion.

Iraq's economic and social problems will continue well beyond 2010, even under the best of circumstances. Also, Iraq can approach the progress it needs to make only if it is not crippled by loan repayments that are well in excess of $100 billion and reparations claims that are even larger.

CHAPTER THREE

THE STRATEGIC CONTEXT
OF THE WAR IN IRAQ

Lessons of history are important to remember when addressing strategic consequences of U.S. actions in Iraq. Consequences cannot be measured by what the United States can accomplish between now and 2005—or by the time the United States transfers all power and decision-making to a new Iraqi government. Consequences will be measured by the outcome after the United States transfers sovereignty and leaves. The test of history is not 2005, but 2010, 2020, and beyond.

Americans therefore need to remember that much will depend on the broader strategic context of matters in the Middle East and the Islamic world—and that this context will not only shape the strategic outcome of events in Iraq, but also in Afghanistan, the war on terrorism, and the Arab-Israeli conflict.

The Iraq War and the nation building that follows will play out in a region with massive demographic and economic challenges.

POPULATION GROWTH

The Middle East and North Africa are a long-term demographic nightmare and must come to grips with their population growth. The U.S. Census Bureau estimates that the population of the Middle East–North Africa region will nearly double between 2004 and 2030. The total population of the Middle East and North Africa grew from 78.7 million in 1950 to 305.7 million in 2000. It could be as high as 624 million in 2050.

Some of the most important, and sometimes troubled, countries in the region will experience explosive population growth. Algeria is

Population Growth in the Middle East–North Africa Region, 1950–2050 (est.)

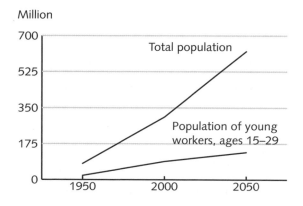

expected to grow from 31 million in 2000 to 53 million in 2050. Egypt has a lower population growth rate than many of its neighbors but is projected to grow from 68 million in 2000 to 113 million in 2050. Gaza is projected to grow from 1.1 to 4.2 million, and the West Bank from 2.2 to 5.6 million during the same period. Iran is estimated to grow from 65 to 100 million, and Iraq from 23 to 57 million. Morocco is projected to grow from 30 to 51 million. Oman will grow from 2.5 to 8.3 million. Saudi Arabia will grow from 22 to 91 million, and Syria from 16 to 34 million. Yemen's population growth rate is so explosive that it is projected to grow from 18 to 71 million.

Population growth is creating a youth explosion that will increase the size of the young working-age population, aged 15 to 29, from 20.5 million in 1950 to 89.2 million in 2000, and 133.7 million in 2050, a social issue compounded by a lack of jobs and job growth, practical work experience, and competitiveness.

Emigration from the region is being driven by these forces and creates new challenges of its own. The *Arab Human Development Report 2003*, published by the United Nations Development Program, cites surveys in which 50 percent of the young Arab males surveyed stated their career plan was to emigrate.

Demographic and economic pressures are only part of the story. Tremendous cultural, societal, political, and ideological pressures exist.

Almost all countries in the region have serious ethnic and religious differences as well as suffer from educational, tribal, and class hierarchies.

WATER

Population growth places demands on infrastructure and water. While the population demands services in the fast-growing urban areas and in the educational systems, the increasing population is exhausting natural water supplies in many countries, leading to growing dependence on desalination and permanent dependence on food imports. Demand for water already exceeds the supply in nearly half the countries in the Middle East and North Africa, and annual renewable water supplies per capita have fallen by 50 percent since 1960 and are projected to fall from 1,250 cubic meters today to 650 cubic meters in 2025—about 14 percent of today's global average. Groundwater is being overpumped and "fossil water" depleted. The region is already critically dependent on food imports.

LAGGING ECONOMIES

Problems of employment and education will challenge regional stability. Some 70 percent of the population is already under 30 years of age, and some 50 percent is under 20. Unemployment, both real and disguised, averages at least 25 percent for young males; no real statistics exist for women; and the number of young people entering the workforce each year will double between now and 2025—all leading to an immense bow wave of future strains on social, educational, political, and economic systems.

For more than two decades, the Middle East and North Africa have had limited or no real growth in per capita income and growing inequity in the distribution of that income. Growth in per capita income in constant prices dropped from 3.6 percent during 1971–1980 to −0.6 percent during 1981–1990, and growth was only 1 percent during 1991–2000. During this entire 30-year period, the disparity between the incomes of rich and poor tended to increase.

Growth of gross domestic product (GDP) is far too low. The World Bank's report on global economic development for 2003 shows a sharp

Comparison of Rates of Growth in Per Capita Income

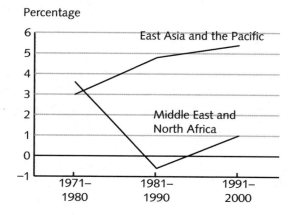

Percentage

decline in economic growth in GDP in constant prices, from 6.5 percent during 1971–1980, to 2.5 percent during 1981–1990. Although growth rose to 3.2 percent during 1991–2000, this rate barely kept pace with population growth.

The Middle East–North Africa region is not competitive with the leading developing regions. Interregional comparisons may be somewhat unfair, but, in fact, economic growth in East Asia and the Pacific was 6.6 percent during 1971–1980, 7.3 percent during 1981–1990, and 7.7 percent during 1991–2000. The growth in real per capita income in East Asia and the Pacific was 3.0 percent during 1971–1980, 4.8 percent during 1981–1990, and 5.4 percent during 1991–2000.

The region is not competitive in trade. Its share of the world's gross national product (GNP) and world trade has declined for nearly a half century; intraregional trade remains limited; and almost all states in the region bypass other states in the region when it comes to trade— their major trading partners are outside the region. The rhetoric of Arab unity and regional development has little relation to reality.

Radical economic changes are affecting societies of the region. Agricultural and rural communities have given way to hyperurbanization and slums. Most countries are now net food importers and must devote a growing portion of their limited water supplies to urban and indus-

Comparison of Rates of Growth in Gross Domestic Product

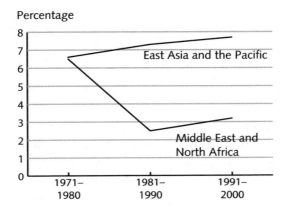

Percentage

trial use. The region cannot eliminate dependence on food imports at any foreseeable point in the future, and the increasing population and water problems are forcing economic and social change.

Oil wealth has always been relative and can no longer sustain any country in the region except Qatar, the United Arab Emirates, and possibly Kuwait. Real per capita oil wealth is now only about 15 percent to 30 percent of its peak in 1980. For example, Saudi Arabia's per capita petroleum exports in 2002 were less than 10 percent of their peak value —in 1980 per capita petroleum exports were $24,000; in 2002, $2,300.

Despite decades of reform plans and foreign aid, no globally competitive economies exist in any of the 23 Middle East–North Africa states. Productivity has been inhibited by problems in education, barriers erected by government bureaucracies, a focus on state industry, a lack of incentives for foreign direct investment, a strong incentive to place domestic private capital in investments outside the region, limitations on women that sharply affect productivity gain, and corruption. Change is beginning in nations like Tunisia, Jordan, and Dubai, but there are no real successes yet. Many states have little more than ambitious plans.

Far too many countries in the region have sustained debt and budget crises. Most states already cannot afford many of the expenditures they should make or have national budgets under great strain. They have cut back on entitlements and investment in infrastructure and have allowed state industries to decline. At the same time, many of these countries still spend far too much on military forces, fail to effectively modernize their forces, and now must spend more on internal security.

CULTURE

The Middle East and North Africa is a region with a long history of failed secularism. Pan Arabism, Arab socialism, the cult of the leader, and exploitative capitalism have all had their day and failed. Most states have patriarchic and authoritarian leaders, one or no real political parties, and elites unprepared for truly representative government. Far too often democracy is a word instead of a practical option.

In far too many cases, the symbols of Western materialism are unaccompanied by any matching values, and, in any case, they are largely unaffordable. At the same time, vast changes in communications—the satellite television news channels like Al Jazeera and the regional content of the Internet—can produce great cultural alienation.

This alienation is compounded by the Arab-Israeli conflict, the military dominance and intervention of the United States, and the often careless and extreme U.S. and Western criticism of Islam and the Arab world. The image of crusaders, neoimperialism, and Western contempt and disregard for the values of the region and the Islamic world are grossly exaggerated. So is the blame assigned to Israel and to the United States for supporting Israel. It is, however, a reality in terms of regional perceptions, and enough elements of truth underlie these perceptions to caution Americans not to ignore them.

It is not surprising, therefore, that many in the region have returned to what they regard as their roots in Islam and ethnicity. They see their future in terms of religion and a broad Arab identity mixed with reliance on extended family and tribe. The inevitable result is extremism, anger, hatred, and violence.

It is equally unsurprising that U.S. calls for reform and democracy are perceived as outside interference motivated by selfish U.S. interests or even Zionist plots, and that U.S. efforts at nation building are greeted with countless conspiracy theories and much suspicion.

This mix of complex forces can—and must—be changed over time. It cannot, however, be changed by overthrowing one dictator or by defeating one leading group of terrorists. It cannot be solved by simply calling for democracy, any more than it can be solved with economic reform without political or social reform.

CHAPTER FOUR

U.S. DRIVE FOR SECURITY

The U.S. intervention in Iraq, like the U.S. role in the war in Afghanistan, the broader struggle against terrorism, and the Arab-Israel conflict, must be seen in the context of continuing regionwide problems that will take at least 10 to 20 years to resolve and that are spilling over into Central, South, and East Asia.

SOCIAL AND ECONOMIC PROBLEMS

The history of the modern Middle East shows that the impact of economic and social problems varies according to national tendencies. No one can deny that Arab and Islamic cultures are powerful regional forces, or that the rhetoric of Arab unity still has great strength. History, however, shows most demographic, social, economic, and political problems play out at a national level. Solutions are found, or not found, one nation at a time; history provides little evidence since the time of Egypt's Gamal Abdel Nasser that any one nation may serve as a transforming example for others.

The movements shaping the Middle East–North Africa region are far too powerful to dissipate quickly or be deeply influenced by a single case, but this does not make short-term U.S. success in Iraq unimportant. Regardless of how well or how badly the United States does in Iraq—and in its three other ongoing wars—it faces decades in which:

- Internal tensions will lead to violence in many states.

- Demographic momentum will increase demographic pressure on almost every nation in the region for at least the next three decades.

- Economic reform will come slowly, particularly for the poor and insufficiently educated.

- Political evolution may succeed over time, but no foundation yet exists for sudden democracy or political reform. Stable political parties, the rule of law, human rights, willingness to compromise and cede power, and the checks and balances that Western republics use to balance internal centers of power are still weak. Attempts at reform that outpace the ability of societies to generate internal change will lead to revolution and new—and usually worse—forms of authoritarianism or theocracy.

- Islamic extremism and terrorism may never come to dominate more than a handful of states, but they will mutate and endure for decades after Osama bin Laden and Al Qaeda are gone. Only sheer luck will prevent them from dominating at least some states or at least posing a critical challenge to some regimes.

- Anger and jealousy at the West, and the United States in particular, may fade if the United States can find a way to help end the Arab-Israeli conflict and achieve enough success in Iraq to ensure that it is not perceived as a group of modern crusaders and an occupying enemy. However, the anger will not disappear and may well be compounded by the backlash from cultural conflicts over emigration and a steadily growing gap between the wealth of the West and the living standards in much of the Middle East and North Africa.

The fact that the future of Iraq and the Middle East will be as difficult, as complex, and as time consuming as its past does not mean that the United States can disengage from the region; neither will the facts that U.S. influence will be far more limited than Americans might like, that reform and change will be driven by local values and priorities, and that there will often be setbacks and reversals.

The United States is not involved in a clash of civilizations. It is, however, on the periphery of a clash within a civilization that affects vital U.S. strategic interests, that can lash out in the form of terrorism and extremist attacks, and that deserves an active U.S. role on moral and humanitarian grounds. Just as the United States did not stand aside during the Cold War, it cannot stand aside now, although engagement may again lead to a half century of challenges and mean the United States can neither fully foresee nor shape the future.

Like it or not, the United States is involved in a war of ideas and values in the Arab and Islamic worlds, with no easy protective barriers between itself and the Middle East, the general threat of Islamic extremism, the Arab-Israeli conflict, the war in Afghanistan, and instability in Central and South Asia. The United States will be a target regardless of how active it is in the region. The events of 9/11 have made part of the threat as obvious as the previous points have shown the need for outside aid and encouragement. Terrorism can reach anywhere in the world, and it sometimes will.

Big quote.

WEAPONS PROLIFERATION

The problem of proliferation goes far beyond Iraq. Iran, Israel, and Syria are active proliferators, and Libya's ultimate intentions remain uncertain. Technology has already flowed in from many other countries, including Pakistan. Proliferation has been a focus of terrorist groups like Al Qaeda, and the flow of technology currently favors the proliferators. It is not possible to address all of the emerging technical challenges that will make proliferation a more serious problem, but key trends include:

- Chemical weapons technology is becoming steadily more available in dual-use form, knowledge of weaponization is spreading, and fourth-generation weapons present a future threat:
  - Steady dissemination of civil and dual-use equipment that can be used to produce chemical weapons, ranging from insecticides to industrial chemicals;
  - Dissemination of technology for advanced persistent nerve gases and fourth-generation chemical weapons;
  - Creation of civil production facilities with legitimate civilian uses that can be converted rapidly or covertly to weapons production;

- Improved tunneling, excavation, and construction capabilities for building underground or covert facilities;
- Dissemination of civil and dual-use environmental and safety equipment that can be used to better conceal trace activities that might reveal proliferation; and
- Broad dissemination of satellite weather data and other data that can be used to improve the employment of chemical weapons.

- Biological weapons technology is becoming far more lethal and easier to acquire:
  - Steady dissemination of civil and dual-use equipment that can be used to produce biological weapons, including large-scale biomedical facilities, pharmaceutical plants, and fermentation facilities;
  - Dissemination of technology for genetic engineering;
  - Better understanding in developing countries of methods of tailoring diseases to alter their levels of infectivity, cycles of infection, and resistance to standard treatments;
  - Creation of civilian production facilities with legitimate civilian uses that can be rapidly or covertly converted to weapons production;
  - Improved tunneling, excavation, and construction capabilities for the creation of underground or covert facilities;
  - Dissemination of civilian and dual-use environmental and safety equipment that can be used to better conceal trace activities that might reveal proliferation and also deal with biological contamination if an attack occurs; and
  - Broad dissemination of satellite weather data and other data that can be used to improve the employment of biological weapons.

- Nuclear weapons remain a major technological and systems integration problem, but design and construction problems are easing and centrifuge technology is becoming more effective and easier to acquire:

– Major advances in computers and commercial or dual-use test equipment that can be used to design weapons and carry out nonfissile tests and simulations, greatly reducing the need for the actual testing of fission and possibly boosted weapons;

– Dissemination of difficult-to-control components that can be adapted for triggering nuclear weapons and manufacturing high-explosive lens;

– Dissemination of centrifuge technology and dual-use materials, and advances in centrifuge designs providing steadily greater capacity;

– Option of creating small, dispersed centrifuge facilities and small folded centrifuges;

– Better understanding in developing countries of the ability to use materials not normally classified as weapons-grade materials to produce fissile events;

– Improved tunneling, excavation, and construction capabilities for the creation of underground or covert facilities; and

– Dissemination of civil and dual-use environmental and safety equipment that can be used to better conceal trace activities that might reveal proliferation.

■ Delivery systems technology for cruise missiles, line source attacks, and covert attacks is becoming steadily more available:

– Growing commercial availability of components for cruise missiles, unmanned aerial vehicles (UAVs), and aircraft conversions;

– Growing availability of global positioning system (GPS) and other civilian-use components that can be used to provide guidance systems;

– Dissemination of civilian technology that can be used to detonate weapons automatically at a given location while in transit;

– Better understanding in developing countries of transmission methods for the use of infectious biological weapons;

– Production of conventional explosive bomblets that can be adapted to disseminate chemical and biological agents; and

– Civil production of items—sprayers and air bags, for example —that can be used as nondestructive dissemination devices.

DEPENDENCE ON MIDDLE EAST ENERGY

The United States and its trading partners are also going to become steadily more dependent on a global economy that, in turn, is going to become steadily more dependent on the energy exports from the Middle East. DOE models project that the global economy will require Middle Eastern oil production to more than double by 2020, and Gulf oil exports to more than double as well. The DOE models also assume that coal and nuclear use will increase in large amounts, that natural gas will move throughout the world in vast quantities that increase faster than the movement of oil, that renewables will experience major increases, and that conservation will steadily make the use of energy more efficient.

Gulf oil production must increase sharply to meet world demand. Regardless of Bush administration and congressional debates over energy policy, DOE estimates that the global economy will require Gulf oil production capacity to increase from 22.4 mbd in 2001 to 24.5 mbd in 2005, 28.7 mbd in 2010, 33.0 mbd in 2015, 39.0 mbd in 2020, and 45.2 mbd in 2025. It is expected that all Gulf producers will increase oil production capacity significantly during the forecast period and that Saudi Arabia and Iraq will more than double their current production capacity.

Exports must more than double and flow securely to meet this demand. The Gulf members of the Organization of Petroleum Exporting Countries (OPEC) alone exported an average of 16.9 mbd, or 30 percent of a world total of 56.3 mbd in 2002. If the North African states are included, the exports climb to 19.5 mbd, or 35 percent. The Energy Information Administration (EIA) projects in its 2004 *Annual Energy Outlook* that Persian Gulf producers are expected to account for 45 percent of worldwide trade in oil by 2007—for the first time since the early 1980s. The EIA projects that the Persian Gulf share of worldwide petroleum exports will then increase gradually to 66 percent by 2025. If oil prices are low, the Persian Gulf share of total exports may reach 76 percent by 2025.

U.S. oil imports are only a subset of U.S. strategic dependence on Middle East oil exports. The United States also relies on the overall health of the global economy and indirectly imports large amounts of energy in the form of manufactured goods dependent on Middle East oil. Moreover, oil is a global commodity, and the United States must compete for the global supply on market terms. As a result, it is the global supply of oil exports—not the specific source of U.S. oil at any given time—that determines availability and price for the United States as well as other nations. The United States is also obligated by treaty to share oil exports with other Organization for Economic Cooperation and Development (OECD) states if a major interruption in exports occurs.

U.S. energy imports will rise sharply. The EIA's *Annual Energy Outlook* for 2004 does, however, report that net imports of petroleum accounted for 53 percent of domestic petroleum consumption in 2002. It also estimates that U.S. dependence on petroleum imports will reach 70 percent in 2025 in the reference case, compared with 68 percent, which the agency forecast in 2003. If oil prices are high, imports are expected to be 65 percent; if oil prices are low, imports are estimated at 75 percent. Both estimates are approximately 5 percent higher than they were in the EIA estimate for 2003.

CHAPTER FIVE

SCENARIOS FOR FUTURE U.S. ENGAGEMENT

It is impossible to predict how the combination of nation building, low-intensity combat, and Iraqi efforts to re-create their nation will play out over the short term, but five strategic outcomes are possible after the U.S.-led coalition fully transfers power or is forced to leave.

DEPARTURE THROUGH DISASTER OR "DEFEAT"

This worst case seems very unlikely, but it is possible that some combination of major enemy successes resembling the Marine Corps barracks disaster in Lebanon coupled with popular demands for a U.S. departure could force the United States and its allies to leave under conditions that appear as a major defeat. This would be the worst case. The United States would appear weak and vulnerable to terrorism, and its allies would be deeply discouraged. It would leave a power vacuum in Iraq and encourage extremism and revolution throughout the region.

Yet, even this case cannot be described as a disaster. Saddam would be gone, along with Iraq's conventional threat and near-term ability to proliferate weapons of mass destruction (WMD) and terror. The Iraqis would still have better opportunities than they had under Saddam, Iraq would still need to export as much oil as possible, and America's allies in the region would still need the United States. As in Vietnam, the issue would be how well and how quickly the United States could learn from its mistakes.

DEPARTURE THROUGH REJECTION OR CIVIL CONFLICT

This case also seems unlikely but possible. The United States and its allies cannot stay in Iraq without at least the tolerance of most Shi`ites and the support of the Kurds. The United States cannot impose a political system or economic and legal reform on a people by force, and it cannot attempt armed nation building without the support, or at least the passivity, of most of the population.

If a new, unstable Iraqi government asks the United States and its allies to leave or if a major civil conflict takes place in Iraq, the United States cannot indefinitely maintain its security and aid efforts. Just as the United States in many ways lost the war in Vietnam when it failed to create a viable new government and lost the support of the Buddhist majority, it would "lose the peace" if Iraq is unable to create a stable new structure of government.

U.S. withdrawal under these circumstances would be a reverse and not a disaster. Iraqi rejection of a U.S.-led nation-building effort, failure to make an effective nation-building effort itself, or dissolution into civil war will largely absolve the United States of responsibility without it being a U.S. military defeat. In addition, Iraq's weakness vis-à-vis Iran and Turkey could well cause any new Iraqi regime to eventually find it needs U.S. support and aid. U.S. allies in the region would continue to need U.S. support as well.

DEPARTURE IN 2005–2006 AMID SIGNS OF HOPE

This case—departure in 2005–2006 amid signs of hope, but after Iraqi rejection of any major or continuing U.S. role in Iraq—is more likely than many Americans care to admit. It would occur if a new Iraqi government wanted continued U.S. civil and military aid but placed severe limits on the size of the U.S. presence and the role the United States played as an adviser. It could occur if the transfer of power resulted in the coming to power of Arab, Islamic, or nationalist forces that severely limited the role of the United States. If the new Iraqi government wanted to assert or prove its independence—by reacting to forces like the backlash from the Arab-Israeli conflict, for example—the United States would be tolerated only out of need during the formation of an elected government and the most critical phases of its aid and security activities, but no real friendship or alliance would exist.

Much depends on whether the emergent Iraqi regime holds together after partial U.S. departure, displays a degree of working pluralism and political reform, and makes economic progress. Such a partial departure could be classified as a victory in strategic terms, would put to rest a host of conspiracy theories about U.S. neoimperialism, and would provide real hope for Iraq. This departure would also absolve the United States of responsibility for the nearly certain five to ten years of turmoil upcoming in Iraq.

Success of this scenario would also depend greatly on internationalizing the aid effort, finding Arab and United Nations (UN) help in dealing with political issues, and retaining in some form many core aid programs and reforms the United States has initiated. As in all five scenarios, much would depend on Iraqis' ability to help themselves.

CONTINUING PRESENCE DESPITE TRANSFER OF SOVEREIGNTY IN 2005–2006

This scenario—a total transfer of sovereignty to the Iraqis, but with the United States maintaining a significant and continuing presence in Iraq—is somewhat less probable than the scenario immediately above, but is similar to it. The United States and its allies would remain popular enough (or would be needed enough) to maintain major aid and military roles and sufficient influence and leverage to sustain political and economic reform efforts.

This case is the best case in many ways. The United States continues its strategic influence, but it is certain to be associated with considerable internal instability in Iraq and is likely to be an awkward mix of rewards and punishments vis-à-vis the Iraqi regime. The United States also will not know true popularity. If this situation endures beyond 2007–2008, it will be only because Iraq fails to deal with its economic, political, and security problems. One advantage is that the United States would have the time to do more and be in a position to act. A disadvantage is that the United States would have to act largely on the basis of Iraqi priorities, on Iraqi terms, and at considerable cost while it is perceived as bearing considerable responsibility for the outcome.

TRANSFORMATION OF IRAQ INTO AN IDEAL FOR THE REGION

Regardless of the hopes of various neoconservatives and the good intentions of the optimistic breed of nation builders, this scenario was an absurd hope from the outset and simply will not happen. Iraq is too difficult a challenge in the near and middle term; the region is affected by too many other factors; and the United States will have too limited a span of future control.

Iraq may become an example to other nations over time; but, if so, it will be because Iraqis transform Iraq successfully on their own terms. It will not be because the United States was prepared to help Iraq in nation building, because the new Iraqi government is a mirror image of the United States, or because Iraq becomes a symbol of U.S. values. Transformation will take place through Iraqi use of initial opportunities given by the United States over a decade or so to prove that an Arab Islamic state can be successful on Arab and Islamic terms.

This outcome would be a strategic victory for the United States even if it bore little resemblance to the more grandiose hopes of at least some who felt a victory over Saddam could suddenly transform the Middle East.

CHAPTER SIX

SHAPING THE STRATEGIC OUTCOME IN IRAQ

The United States cannot with certainty choose among these scenarios to ensure "victory" in Iraq, but the United States has every chance of achieving a form of victory if it is persistent, willing to commit the necessary resources, and accepts the real-world limits on what it can do. No one can predict how the combination of nation building, low-intensity combat, and Iraqi efforts to re-create their nation will play out over the short term, but the United States has ten tools it can use to achieve the best strategic outcomes. Since May of 2003, the United States has shown that it is adaptable, and it is already making some use of all these tools.

IRAQ-BASED SOLUTIONS

- **Acceptance of national differences.** Accept the fact that Iraq's interests and solutions differ from those of the United States. Multiculturalism cannot consist of trying to turn different countries with different cultures into mirror images of the United States, and the United States cannot succeed by trying to transform Iraq into its own image. It cannot succeed if it does not allow Iraqis to make their own choices and mistakes and to take over power in every dimension as soon as is practical. Also, the United States cannot succeed if it behaves as if Iraq does not have foreign policy and security interests different from those of the United States.

- **Information.** Shift the approach to information campaigns and efforts to win hearts and minds from a U.S.-centric approach to an Iraqi approach—run by Iraqis. In mid-2004, it is too late for the

31

United States to win Iraqi hearts and minds except through the success of its actions. The United States needs to do everything possible to aid the Iraqis in creating their own media and give the new Iraqi government the tool of broadcast capability to reach the Iraqi people on as pluralist a basis as possible. Iraqi people do not need to hear the Americans speak for the United States; they need to hear Iraqis speak for Iraq.

U.S. REALISM

- **Perseverance.** Stay the course militarily but develop Iraqi security forces as soon as possible. The U.S. military has already shown far more realism and adaptability than it did in Vietnam, and "Iraqization" has already provided more than 200,000 men for military, police, and security forces. The United States and its allies must accept the need to fight the mix of insurgents to the point of defeat; fund the needed mix of military operations, aid, and civil action programs; and create effective Iraqi forces.

The United States must continue to provide all of the necessary low-intensity warfare capabilities and be willing to endure at least one year more of casualties and armed nation building. It certainly means tens, if not hundreds, of billions of dollars of international aid—aid not dependent on mortgaging Iraq's oil—over a period far longer than the next fiscal year. It also means several years of armed nation building.

Americans need to accept that the price tag may be much higher—higher in more than dollars—than the United States now plans. The price tag may well be at least 1,000 U.S. dead. The United States may have to accept the political cost of reaching out to allies and the UN, and even admitting mistakes. Most important, the solution lies in doing as much as possible, as soon as possible, and flooding resources forward even at the cost of waste. Every delay and every exercise in cost-effectiveness mean higher costs and higher risks in the future—and the risks include seeing ordinary Sunnis as well as the Shi`a part of the country turn against the United States.

■ **Flexibility.** Transfer political and administrative power as quickly as possible to Iraqis on Iraqi terms. The United States is already acting on a schedule that goes far to meet Iraqi expectations and is funding vital programs to aid in democratization, legal reform, and human rights. The main challenges will be accepting that Iraq will not, and does not want to, meet many U.S. political expectations and standards; that the new government will not be as favorable as the United States prefers; and that many popularly chosen members may be critical and sometimes hostile. The United States has unleashed internal forces in Iraq that it must live with, and it may well find that many leaders who have come in from exile or who are overtly pro-American are not selected for leadership by the Iraqis. The United States must also be prepared to allow Iraqis to make their own mistakes at every level and do things in the Iraqi way. In general, the United States must accept that the key goals are human rights, the rule of law, and stability in power sharing—not a copy of the U.S. political system.

ECONOMIC ASSISTANCE AND DEVELOPMENT

■ **Generosity.** Maintain a high level of aid, but allow Iraq to reform its economy on its own terms. The United States cannot afford to be cost-effective in its use of aid funds or try to impose its own drastic reforms when Iraqis do not support them. The United States must buy stability and opportunity, not achieve rapid economic transformation.

■ **Debt forgiveness.** Must make sustained efforts to win forgiveness of Iraqi debts and reparations and bring in other countries and businesses that are willing to help. The United States must not seek to advance U.S. interests only.

■ **Economic development.** Ensure energy investment and development on Iraqi terms. The United States already seems to have given up any efforts to rapidly privatize the Iraqi oil industry or "securitize" Iraq's economic recovery and reform through U.S. efforts to mortgage Iraqi oil. Iraqis have the capability to manage Iraq's energy development on their terms and should be allowed to do so in a free and competitive manner; it is the Iraqis who should negotiate new contracts for exploration, oil field development, and downstream projects.

CONTINUING ENGAGEMENT

- **Patience.** Plan now for five more years of continued engagement after full Iraqi sovereignty. Even in the worst-case scenario—departure after disaster—the United States will still have to deal with Iraq on some basis. In all of the other scenarios, and perhaps even in the worst-case scenario, it will need a strong embassy staff that can assist Iraq with aid at the security, political, and economic levels; encourage foreign investment; and respond to emergency needs and crises. The United States cannot control Iraq's future, but it can influence it and help Iraq achieve its own goals. This almost certainly means a significant foreign aid program until at least 2010. The United States certainly must not react to perceived Iraqi hostility by severing relations, enforcing new sanctions legislations, or taking any measures that cut the United States off from an Iraq that may well evolve toward a more favorable regime and relationship.

- **Neighbors.** Long-term U.S. policy in the Gulf does not and will not hinge on Iraq. The United States must pursue its broader interests in the region. In doing so, however, it must remember that Iraq's future depends heavily on the roles played by U.S. friends and allies—Jordan, Kuwait, Turkey, and Saudi Arabia—to help Iraq and avoid interference in Iraq's internal affairs that could trigger new problems. The United States must also be prepared to work with Iran and Syria when this is productive and pressure them when pressure is the only alternative. The United States must recognize that it cannot count on Iraq to transform the region; instead, the United States must work to ensure that Iraq is safe from the region and that it receives as much aid as possible.

- **World community.** Engage the UN and international community. The United States cannot preserve control over Iraq's destiny;

in fact, it has never actually controlled Iraq. It can defuse much of the tension that now exists between Iraq and the United States, however, by broadening the basis of international aid and support as quickly as possible and expanding the security mission to include NATO and other international participants.

CHAPTER SEVEN

STRATEGY
AND
RISK OF STRATEGIC OVERREACH

In fairness to the Bush administration, only one of the four wars the United States now faces—the war in Iraq—can be called optional (see chapter eight). Afghanistan came as the result of a major attack on the United States. The problem of terrorism had arisen long before September 11, 2001; and U.S. involvement in Arab-Israeli conflicts is inevitable unless a true and lasting peace can be achieved or the United States abandons an ally.

And Iraq is thought optional largely in retrospect. The Bush administration and, in England, the Blair government may have politicized some aspects of the assessment of Iraqi proliferation, but almost all experts felt the threat was more serious than it has proved to be. Moreover, Saddam Hussein's Iraq would likely have triggered another regional conflict in the future, just as most of Iraq's present internal problems would have surfaced even if the United States, Britain, and Australia had never invaded.

The United States in 2004 does not face the resulting possibility of fighting two major regional contingencies, which had been the strategic focus of both the first Bush administration and the Clinton administration. The United States faces instead the reality of actually fighting three low-intensity conflicts as well as its deep strategic involvement in a fourth. Moreover, the United States still faces the risk of involvement in additional major regional conflicts such as in Iran, North Korea, Taiwan, and Columbia.

U.S. military planning and strategy must be reevaluated in terms of current U.S. involvement in four conflicts and in the face of lessons that grow out of U.S. experience in Iraq and that apply to other wars as well.

STRATEGIC ENGAGEMENT AND OBJECTIVES

Strategic engagement requires objective—not ideological—assessments of the problems to be handled and the size and cost of the effort necessary to achieve decisive grand strategic results. Neither a strategy based on capabilities nor a strategy based on theoretical sizing contingencies is meaningful when real-world conflicts and well-defined contingencies require a strategy and force plan that can deal with reality rather than theory. The United States must constantly adapt its strategy, policy, and military forces to the tasks at hand and those it can immediately foresee. The United States cannot base practical plans on hopes, strategic slogans, ideology, or on the idea it can control or predict the future.

The United States must limit new strategic adventures where possible, and it needs to avoid additional military commitments and conflicts unless they serve vital strategic interests. Regardless of the outcome of the recommended reevaluation of force transformation, it will take at least two to three years before the United States can create major new force elements and military capabilities; some changes will require at least five to ten years.

The United States already faces serious strategic overstretch, and nothing could be more dangerous than assuming that existing problems can be solved by adding new ones—such as Syria or Iran. Deterrence, containment, and diplomacy—in other words, a new emphasis on international action and allies as substitutes for U.S. forces—are imperative for avoiding additional military commitments.

The United States must pursue strategies and tactics that reflect the fact that many of its current conflicts cannot be resolved by defeating a well-defined enemy; many of today's conflicts involve political, social, and economic forces that will take years, if not decades, to run their course. At best, Iraq will be an unstable and evolving state for a decade after the United States leaves. At worst, it could be the target of strong anti-U.S. feelings in the Gulf region and Arab world.

The war in Afghanistan is mutating in ways that are beyond U.S. control, and nation building thus far is failing. The U.S. war on terrorism is not a war against Al Qaeda but against violent Islamic extremism driven by mass demographic, economic, and social forces in a region with limited political legitimacy. It may take a quarter of a century to prevail in the war on terrorism. The Israeli-Palestinian conflict seems years away from peace, and the most recent peace process has shown how tenuous and uncertain even a seemingly successful peace process can be.

INTERNATIONALISM

"Superpower" has always been a dangerous term, and, although it may not be a misnomer, it certainly does not imply U.S. freedom of action. The resulting exaggeration of U.S. capabilities and strategic focus on bipolar threats and peer rivals miss the point. The United States faces the problem of being a global power with limited resources—a problem that Great Britain faced throughout the nineteenth century. The world already is multipolar, with severe limits to what the United States can do and how many places it can do it. Coalitions and alliances are more important than ever.

COALITIONS

The United States has no alternative to internationalism. At times the United States may disagree with the UN or allies, but U.S. strategy must be based on seeking consensus wherever possible, compromise when necessary, and coalitions that underpin nearly every action. U.S. rhetoric can no longer be parochial or driven by domestic politics; it must take full account of the values and sensitivities of others.

U.S. military strategy must give interoperability and military advisory efforts the same priority it gives the concept of jointness. To lead, the United States must also learn to follow. We must never subordinate our vital national interests to others, but this will rarely be the issue in practice. Instead, the challenges will be to subordinate arrogance to the end of achieving true partnerships and to shape diplomacy to create lasting coalitions of willing partners rather than coalitions of the pressured and intimidated.

Great as U.S. power is, it cannot substitute for coalitions and every possible effective use of international organizations. Most nongovernmental organizations (NGOs) and international organizations are not organized for armed nation building, and they would face severe—if not crippling—limitations if they were targeted in a low-intensity combat environment or by large-scale terrorism.

NATION BUILDING

Armed nation building is a challenge only the United States is currently equipped to meet. Although allies, the UN, and NGOs can help in many aspects of security and nation-building operations, they often cannot operate on the scale required to deal with nation building in the midst of resolute low-intensity combat. Armed nation building requires continuing U.S. military and security efforts as well as civil and economic aid programs. Security and nation building require not only new forms of U.S. rapid deployment but also major financial resources and the development of new approaches to providing economic aid and the necessary contract support.

DETERRENCE AND CONTAINMENT

Deterrence and containment are more complex than they were at the time of the Cold War, but they still are critical tools; and their success also depends on formal and informal alliances. The need to create reliable structures of deterrence must also respond to the reality of weapons proliferation—which is no longer how to prevent proliferation but rather how to live as safely as possible with it.

The United States needs to restructure its land and air forces into a force mix that is more mobile, better tailored to rapid reaction, and better suited to asymmetric warfare. It needs better staging points for power projection in areas where the United States has limited basing and facilities, and it needs an enhanced capability to prevail in the low-intensity combat—with its emphasis on light forces and human intelligence (HUMINT) operations rather than heavy forces and high technology—that is dominated by terrorists and hostile movements.

Military intervention cannot be the dominant means of exercising U.S. military power; better ways must be found to use the threat of U.S. military power to deter and contain asymmetric conflicts and new political and economic threats. War avoidance is just as important in the post–Cold War era as it was during the Cold War.

WAR AND DIPLOMACY

War must be an extension of diplomacy by other means, but, in turn, diplomacy must be an extension of war by other means. U.S. security strategy must be based on the understanding that diplomacy, peace negotiations, and arms control are also an extension of—and substitute for—war by other means. It is easy for a superpower to threaten force, but it is far harder to use it; and bluffs get called. Fighting should be a last resort, and all possible means must be used to limit the number of fights.

STABILIZATION

Military victory in asymmetric warfare can be virtually meaningless without successful nation building at the political, economic, and security levels. Stabilization operations—Phase IV operations—are far more challenging than fighting conventional military forces. Stabilization also probably can be conducted best if the United States is prepared for immediate action after the defeat of conventional enemy forces. In both Afghanistan and Iraq, the United States wasted critical days, weeks, and months when it failed to engage in a security effort before opposition movements could regroup and reengage. U.S. actions caused a power vacuum because the United States was not prepared for nation building and the escalation of resistance after enemy conventional forces were defeated.

The Quadrennial Defense Review (QDR) was correct in stressing the risk that asymmetric warfare poses to the United States in spite of its conventional strength. The QDR failed, however, to look beyond the narrow definition of the problems of direct combat to the problems of containment and deterrence, conflict termination, and armed nation building. Many of today's problems in Iraq stem from the fact that the

Defense Department and the Bush administration were as badly prepared for conflict termination, nation building, and low-intensity
threats after the defeat of Saddam's regular military forces as they were
well prepared to effect that defeat.

The price tag for stabilization involves more than dollars and includes some share of responsibility for every U.S. body bag flown out of
Iraq. To a lesser degree, the same is true of the situation in Afghanistan.
The problem is scarcely new. The United States failed at both nation
building and Vietnamization in Vietnam. It failed in Lebanon in the
early 1980s. It failed in Haiti, and it failed in Somalia. The stakes, levels
of involvement, and costs to the United States may have been far lower
in some of these cases, but the fact remains that the United States failed.

MANPOWER SKILLS

Force transformation cannot be dominated by technology; manpower
skills, not technology, are the key. The Afghan War emphasized air
power, which could not secure the country or defeat the Taliban and Al
Qaeda forces that were able to mutate and disperse quickly. The Iraq
War began with heavy conventional land forces and soon became a
heavy air-land battle. Through late April 2003, it comprised air power;
armor; intelligence, surveillance, and reconnaissance (IS&R); and precision. It showed that high-technology forces could decisively defeat
lower-technology conventional forces without much regard for force
numbers and the force ratios critical in past conflicts. Since the fall of
Saddam's regime, however, the United States has been forced to rein-
vent the way in which it uses its forces in Iraq. Technology and an emphasis on destroying enemy hard targets and major weapons systems
failed when the problem became conflict termination, armed nation
building, and low-intensity warfare.

The military missions of low-intensity combat, economic aid, civil-
military relations, security, and information campaigns are manpower
dominated, and they require skilled military manpower as well as new
forms of civil expertise in other departments as well. HUMINT can still
be more important than technical collection; local experience and language skills are critical; and the ability to use aid dollars can be more
important than the ability to use bullets.

This requires a fundamental reexamination of U.S. force plans and force transformation concepts. For decades, the United States has sought to use technology as a substitute for defense spending, for force numbers, and for manpower numbers. In fact, during the conventional phases of the campaigns in both Afghanistan and Iraq, acquisition of transformational technology was seen as permitting further force and manpower cuts and therefore achieving additional savings in defense spending.

Although technology has been, is, and will be critical to U.S. power and military success, it is correct to question whether the United States has any credible way of using technology to further cut forces and manpower without taking unacceptable risks. Creating the proper mix of capabilities for asymmetric warfare, low-intensity conflict, security and Phase IV operations, and nation building requires large numbers of skilled and experienced personnel. Technology at best aids—and does not substitute for—force size and manpower numbers.

This problem is compounded by the fact that the United States does not now have under development a single major transformational weapons system or technology that seems likely to be delivered on time, with the promised effectiveness, at even half of the unit-life-cycle cost originally promised. During the past quarter century, the United States has made little meaningful progress in the effective planning and management of the development and procurement of advanced military technology—the ability to integrate technology into realistic budgets and force plans. Although the United States has shown it can transform, it has not shown it can plan and manage transformation.

For at least the next half decade, the United States must also confront the backlog of maintenance and service requirements created by its operations in Iraq and Afghanistan as well as retain and modernize far greater numbers of its so-called legacy systems that it had planned.

LIMITS OF TECHNOLOGY

Technology-based force transformation and the revolution in military affairs are tools with severe and sometimes crippling limits. The ability to provide IS&R coverage of the world is of immense value. IS&R does not, however, provide the ability to understand the world, deal with complex political issues, fight effectively in the face of terrorism and many forms of low-intensity conflict and asymmetric warfare, manage conflict termination and peacemaking, and protect nation building.

The ability to make use of precision weapons, helicopter mobility, and armor to destroy enemy conventional forces and blow up fixed targets around the clock is also of great tactical value, but it does not mean that defeating enemy's conventional forces really wins wars. The United States is still as bad as it was in World War II at knowing what to blow up in strategic targeting and many aspects of interdiction bombing.

There are also good reasons to question whether many aspects of "net-centric" warfare are simply little more than a conceptual myth that conceals the military equivalent of the Emperor's new clothes in the impenetrability of incomprehensible PowerPoint® slides that cannot be translated into procurable systems, workable human interfaces, and affordable Future Year Defense Programs.

In practice, there is a need to make more effective use of legacy systems and evolutionary improvements in weapons and technology to support "human-centric" forms of military action that require extensive HUMINT and area skills, high levels of training and experience, and effective leadership in not only defeating the enemy in battle but also winning the peace. There is a need to create military forces with extensive experience in civil-military action in addition to forces that can use aid as effectively as weapons—dollars as well as bullets. It also means redefining interoperability to recognize that low-tech allied forces engaged in nation building, civil-military affairs missions, and security missions can often be as effective as, or more effective than, high-tech U.S. forces.

JOINTNESS

Jointness cannot be a simple issue of restructuring the U.S. military; it is far broader than the military. Jointness must occur within the entire executive branch, on a civil-military level as well as on a military-military level.

The Iraq War has shown that the Bush administration's assent to small cadres in the Office of the Secretary of Defense, the Office of the

Vice President, and the National Security Council permitted ideologues to bypass the U.S. national security process in ways that led to critical failures in key strategic tasks like conflict termination and nation building. More broadly, similar failures have occurred in almost every aspect of U.S. strategic engagements and diplomacy, including the critical areas of counterproliferation and the Arab-Israeli peace process.

To date, this lack of jointness in the Bush administration's national security team has effected a Department of Defense–driven breakdown in the interagency process similar to that during the period in which critical decisions were made to carry out the massive U.S. buildup in Vietnam.

An advisory national security affairs adviser is a failed national security affairs adviser; effective leadership is required to force coordination on the U.S. national security process. Unresolved conflicts between leaders like Secretary of State Colin L. Powell and Secretary of Defense Donald H. Rumsfeld, the exclusion of other cabinet members from key tasks, insufficient review of military planning, and the bestowal of too much power on small elements within given departments have weakened U.S. efforts and needlessly alienated U.S. allies. The creation of a large and highly ideological foreign policy staff in the vice president's office is a further anomaly in the interagency process.

The U.S. interagency process simply cannot function with such loosely defined roles, a lack of formal checks and balances, and a largely advisory national security affairs adviser. Jointness must go far beyond the military; it must apply to all national security operations.

COMPLEXITY

Policy, analysis, and intelligence must accept the truth that the world is complex, deal with complexity honestly and objectively, and seek evolution and oppose revolution.

The United States is currently involved in four complex wars (see chapter eight), each of which requires the most objective intelligence and analysis possible. There is no room for ideological sound bites and overly simplistic solutions, and force transformation cannot cut any mystical Gordian knot. The United States cannot afford to rush into—

or stay in—any conflict on ideological grounds; and it cannot afford to avoid any necessary commitment because of idealism. The United States needs to act on informed pragmatism.

One recommendation is to stop oversimplifying and sloganizing—and cease in particular any mirror imaging and assuming that democratization is the solution, or even first priority, for every country. The United States needs to deal with security threats quietly and objectively on a country-by-country and movement-by-movement basis.

As the United States seeks reform in the Near East and North Africa, it must understand that progress in economic development, higher living standards of the ordinary citizen, population issues, and human rights improvements can be more important in the near term than progress toward elections. In fact, democracy could be purposeless, or even destructive, without viable political parties, political leaders capable of moving their nations toward moderation and economic development, and enough national consensus to include different ethnic, ideological, and religious factions in a stable pluralistic structure. Also, the United States must understand that other societies and cultures can move toward political, social, and economic modernization on a route different from one the United States at first envisions.

The United States cannot afford to be careless and abuse words like "Islam" and "Arab" or, in another region, ignore the sensitivities of key allies like South Korea in dealing with threats from North Korea. It cannot afford to alienate its European allies or lose support in the UN by throwing nations like Iran into an imaginary axis of evil. It needs nations like Saudi Arabia as allies in the struggle against movements like Al Qaeda. It also cannot afford to confuse terrorist movements driven by largely neo-Salafi beliefs with different movements such as the Wahhabi sect of Islam, any more than it can afford to act as if Al Qaeda alone somehow dominates a far more complex mix of threats than it really does.

The United States needs a nuanced pragmatism that deals with each nation and each threat individually and in proportion to the actual threat. It must give regional and other allies an appropriate role and influence in decisionmaking instead of bullying them with ideology and rhetoric. It needs to engage the checks and balances of the full interagency process and of area and intelligence professionals, and it also needs to seek a bipartisan approach with proper consultation with the Congress.

ORGANIZATIONAL REFORM

Stabilization, armed nation building, and peacemaking require a new approach to organizing U.S. government efforts.

No one knows when the United States will have to repeat stabilization and nation-building activities on the level of Iraq. For Iraq, the civilian agencies of the U.S. government were not adequately prepared to analyze and plan for the political, security, aid, and information programs needed in Iraq and to provide staff with suitable training and ability to operate in a high-threat environment. The State Department was prepared to analyze the challenges, but it lacked both planning and operational capability and staff prepared to work in the field in a combat environment.

The integration of the U.S. Agency for International Development into the Department of State has compounded the problems of U.S. aid efforts because U.S. agencies previously transferred many generic aid functions to the World Bank and the International Monetary Fund. No staff had been prepared, sized, and trained to deal with nation building on the scale of Iraq, neither could they formulate and administer the massive aid program required. Contractors were overburdened with large-scale contracts because these were the easiest contracts to grant and administer in spite of contractors' lack of experience in a command economy and a high-threat environment. U.S. government and contractor staff—often with limited experience—had to be swiftly recruited for three- to twelve-month tours, a period too short to ensure continuity in such missions.

It is a tribute to the Coalition Provisional Authority and everyone involved that so much could be done despite the lack of effective planning and preparation before the end of major combat operations against Iraq's conventional forces. This deficit of planning should never happen again, however. Denial of the importance and scale of the mission before the event in no way prevents it from being necessary when reality intervenes.

The National Security Council, the Department of State, and the Department of Defense must be capable of mounting security and nation-building missions, whether these are called postconflict, Phase IV, stabilization, or reconstruction missions. The United States must have the tools to win a peace just as it has them to win a war—to provide security after the termination of a conflict and to support nation building by creating viable political systems, economic stability and growth, effective military and security forces, a public information system, and a free press. Thus, the National Security Council must have expertise, the Department of State must have operational capability, the Department of Defense must have military capability; other agencies need to be ready to provide support.

The United States must never repeat its most serious mistakes in Iraq and Afghanistan. From the start, security and nation building must be a fundamental part of the planning and execution of military operations that are directed at foreign governments. Nation-building and security operations must be clear before military operations begin, costs and risks should be fully assessed, Congress should be consulted as it is before military operations, and necessary resources should be available. As combat proceeds, security and nation building must also proceed, with no pauses that create a power vacuum.

MILITARY COOPERATION

The United States needs to rethink its arms sales and security policies. It is still selling massive amounts of arms to the Middle East–North Africa region, with more attention paid to the dollar value of sales than to their impact on local societies, the need for interoperability and effectiveness, and changes in security needs that increasingly focus on internal security.

The United States signed new arms sales agreements worth $13.3 billion with Middle Eastern countries during 1995–1998; total sales to the region were $30.8 billion. Most arms purchased from the United States are still in delivery or early conversion and require extensive U.S. advisory and contract support to be effective. The United States signed new arms contracts worth another $17.2 billion during 1999–2002, out of worldwide sales to the region of $35.9 billion. All these latter sales require extensive U.S. advisory and contract support. At present, almost all of these sales are to countries with poorly integrated arms buys and low levels of readiness and sustainability. They also offer only limited interoperability with U.S. forces.

The sheer volume of these sales also does as much to threaten regional security as it does to aid it. The United States needs to pay far more attention to the social and economic needs of countries in the Middle East, and to work with other sellers to reduce the volume of sales. It also needs to work in tandem with regional powers to help them make the arms they do need effective and sustainable, create local security arrangements, and improve interoperability for the purposes of both deterrence and war fighting.

Most countries in the Middle East and North Africa now face internal security threats that are more serious than external threats. The United States needs to recast its security assistance programs to help nations fight more effectively against terrorism and extremism while not abusing human rights or delaying necessary political, social, and economic reforms.

PUBLIC RELATIONS

The United States needs to organize for effective information campaigns at the same time it seeks to create regional and allied campaigns that will influence the Arab and Islamic worlds.

The integration of the U.S. Information Agency into the Department of State and major cutbacks in U.S. information and public diplomacy efforts have deprived the United States of a critical tool that works best when regional efforts are combined with well-funded and well-staffed efforts at the embassy and locally. The United States needs to revitalize its in-country and regional information efforts in a focused and effective way that takes advantage of the tools of satellite broadcasting and the Internet.

The United States, however, can never be an Arab country or an Islamic country. It needs to work with its friends and allies in the region and seek their help in creating information campaigns that reject Islamic radicalism, violence, and terrorism and support reform. The United States should not try to speak for the Arabs or for Islam; it should help people of the region speak for themselves.

INVESTMENT AND FUNDING

The U.S. private sector and international foreign direct investment should be integrated into the U.S. security strategy. Far too often the United States ignores the role that the U.S. private sector can and must play in achieving evolutionary reform. The United States often emphasizes sanctions over trade and economic contact when it deals with hostile or radical states, and it assigns too low a priority to helping the U.S. private sector invest in friendly states. The U.S. government should undertake a zero-based review of how it can encourage private sector activity in the Middle East.

The United States has agonizing decisions to make about defense resources. In spite of recent, major increases in defense spending, the present force plan is unsustainable in the face of the combined funding burdens of operations, modernization, and transformation.

It is obvious that funding in the current Future Years Defense Program does not allow the United States to come close to paying for both its planned force levels and force improvement plans. Everyone with any experience stopped believing in estimated procurement costs long ago. Equally clear, however, is that the United States now faces years of unanticipated conflicts, many involving armed peacemaking and nation building; and it must rethink deterrence in terms of proliferation. This is not simply a matter of billions of dollars; it is a matter of spending several more percentage points of the gross national product of the United States.

INTELLIGENCE REFORM

Current methods of intelligence collection and analysis cannot guarantee adequate preparation for stabilization operations, support low-intensity combat properly, or support the nation-building phase properly.

New Approaches

The United States needs to reassess the fundamentals of its approach to intelligence in order to support adequate planning for the combat termination, security, and nation-building phases of asymmetric warfare and peacemaking operations. Jointness identical to that in the overall interagency process is needed in the intelligence community effort to prepare for asymmetric warfare. Such enhanced jointness would ensure that the analysis provided to policymakers, planners, and operators fully presents the problems and challenges of stabilization and armed nation building. The Department of Defense should never again be able to filter or reject community-wide analysis; and priorities must never again be assigned to intelligence for military operations so that adequate intelligence analysis and support are unready for the stabilization and nation-building phase.

It is equally important that adequate tactical intelligence support—sufficient tactical HUMINT support combined with sufficient area expertise and linguistic skills—be available from the beginning of combat operations to the end of security and nation-building operations. Technology can be a powerful tool, but it is an aid—not a substitute—for the human skills and talents necessary to support low-intensity combat and expand the role of tactical HUMINT, all the while supporting aid efforts, civil-military relations, and combat operations. At the same time, civilian intelligence agency efforts need to be recast to support nation-building and security operations.

Iraq and Afghanistan show that tactical intelligence must operate as part of a team effort with those involved in counterinsurgency operations, the political and economic phases of nation building, and security and military advisory teams.

It is particularly critical that both intelligence and operations directly integrate combat activity with civil-military relations work, U.S. military police and security efforts, economic aid in direct support of low-intensity-combat and security operations, the training of local security forces and their integration into the HUMINT effort, and the creation of effective information campaigns. In the future, this may require a far better integration of military and civil efforts in both intelligence and operations than has occurred in either Iraq or Afghanistan.

Weapons Proliferation

The Iraq war has shown that current methods of intelligence collection and analysis and of arms control and inspection cannot assure an adequate understanding of the risks posed by proliferation. The United States needs to fundamentally reassess its difficulties with intelligence about proliferation and the lessons Iraq provides regarding arms control. Far too much of the media coverage and outside analysis of the intelligence failures in Iraq has focused on the politics of the situation or has implied that intelligence failed because it was improperly managed and reviewed. In fact, there have been long-standing problems in how the CIA managed its counterproliferation efforts, and institutional biases affected almost all intelligence community reporting and analysis on the subject.

The fact remains, however, that practically all of the world's intelligence agencies viewed Iraq as a far more serious proliferator than current evidence supports. Moreover, some ten years of arms inspections by the United Nations Special Commission (UNSCOM), the International Atomic Energy Agency (IAEA), and the United Nations Monitoring, Verification, and Inspection Commission (UNMOVIC) also failed to provide a clear characterization of what Iraq had or had not done.

The reasons for the gaps in intelligence on Iraq can be explained more by the currently unavoidable limits in collection and analysis than by politics or the internal failings of the U.S. intelligence community and its counterparts. These are failures that affect intelligence about other proliferating states like Egypt, India, Iran, Israel, Libya, North Korea, Pakistan, and Syria. Moreover, these failures show an inability to inspect and verify according to current agreements on arms control, a failing far more serious than many other gaps in intelligence.

The issue is not the politics of intelligence in Iraq. The issues are how to best fix a mix of serious problems in the capabilities of the intelligence community to collect and analyze information about proliferation as well as confront the greater challenges of arms control inspection and verification. At a minimum, intelligence must be improved or its limitations and uncertainties must be frankly communicated.

For proliferating countries, arms control is an extension of war by other means. The very nature of arms control agreements like the Nuclear Non-Proliferation Treaty (NPT), the Biological Weapons Convention (BWC), and Chemical Weapons Convention (CWC) encourages proliferating nations to lie and conceal as effectively as possible. The same is true of supplier agreements like the Missile Technology Control Regime (MTCR) and the Australia Group as well as any form of sanctions. Arms control encourages compliance only among nonproliferators and nonsellers, and current enforcement efforts are too weak to be effective while agreement provisions permit nations that succeed in lying and concealing to transfer licensed technology.

The technology of proliferation generally permits research and development (R&D) to be divided into many small facilities and projects, some ostensibly as legitimate civil research and others hidden in civil and commercial facilities. As proliferators become more sophisticated, they learn to create dispersed, redundant, and parallel programs and to mix secret, covert programs with open, civil, or dual-use programs. Chemical, biological, and cruise missile programs are particularly easy to divide into small cells or operations, and this is becoming increasingly true of nuclear weapons centrifuge programs, plutonium processing and fuel cycles, and the testing and simulation of nuclear weapons that do not involve weapons-grade materials. Many key aspects of ballistic missile R&D, including warhead and launch system design, fit into this category.

Iraq and most other proliferators in the past focused on creating stockpiles of weapons for fighting theater conflicts against military forces. Stockpiles require large inventories, large-scale deployments, and combinations of training and war-fighting preparations that create significant intelligence indicators. Many proliferators may now be pursuing other strategies:

- Bring weapons to full development and wait until a threat becomes imminent before actually producing weapons;
- Bring weapons to full development before producing them for an imminent threat, and also create large dual-use civilian facilities—pharmaceutical plants, food-processing plants, breweries, petro-

chemical plants, and pesticide plants—that convert rapidly to the production of WMD; assembly lines can be concealed in other commercial activities, and weapons production facilities can be kept at the ready; and

- Create a few lethal biological or nuclear weapons to attack a foreign country's key political or civilian facilities instead of its military forces; lethal noninfectious or infectious biological agents can be directed at humans, and biological weapons can be directed at crops or livestock.

Countries with inventories of weapons can pursue different strategies. They can disclose and destroy the weapons if they know that the country does not face an urgent war-fighting need, that better weapons are coming, and that destruction suits current political objectives. They can claim to destroy them but instead hide remaining weapons in covert areas known only to a few. They can claim to destroy (while they lie about the destruction) and instead disperse weapons where they can be used for war fighting. Intelligence collection often cannot distinguish among such strategies, and a proliferator like Iraq can pursue a mix of such strategies—depending on the value of the weapon.

In many cases, it cannot be learned with confidence whether a program is for R&D, for weapons production and deployment, or is production capable and breakout oriented. It complicates matters that Iraq and other countries have learned to play a shell game by developing multiple surface and underground military facilities and dual-use facilities and to create relatively mobile mixes of trailer- or vehicle-mounted and palletized equipment for rapid movement. Large special-purpose facilities with difficult-to-move equipment often still exist, but they are no longer the rule. Intelligence collection takes time, and it often lags behind country activities.

There is no clear case other than the worst case. Unless a country keeps accurate records of its programs, it is often easier to estimate the most it can do instead of provide an accurate picture of what it has actually done. This problem of analysis was particularly severe in the case of Iraq, which had systematically lied and concealed its efforts since the late 1970s and had become even more secretive after the Israeli raid on its Osirak reactor in 1981. Iraq had a 20-year track record with U.S. intelligence in which the worst cases turned out to be the real cases. UN-SCOM discovered a massive new Iraqi biological weapons program. Discoveries of lies about weaponizing persistent nerve gas partly led to UNSCOM's expulsion in 1998; and, although UNMOVIC made no major discoveries of chemical, biological, radiological, and nuclear (CBRN) weapons in 2002–2003, it did find new illegal missile programs. The historical pattern in Iraq was just as clear as it was unclear for 9/11, but it reinforced worst-case analysis.

In most cases, it is impossible to know the progress and the degree of success of a project. The history of proliferation is not the history of proliferators overcoming major technical and manufacturing problems; instead, it is the history of massive management and systems integration problems, political failures, lying advocates and entrepreneurs, project managers who hide the truth from their political masters, and occasional sudden successes. Without an intelligence breakthrough, it is rarely possible to assess the success of a given effort. Even on-the-scene inspection can produce wrong results unless a given project can be subjected to detailed technical testing. For example, once UNSCOM and the IAEA fully assessed the efficiency of Iraq's calutron and centrifuge programs, they saw that almost all of their preliminary reporting on Iraq's nuclear effort in 1992–1993 had exaggerated Iraqi capabilities.

Countering most of these collection problems requires a reliable mix of redundant HUMINT sources within the system or as defectors. However, the United States has never claimed or implied it has had such capabilities in any proliferating country; and the history of U.S., British, UNSCOM, and UNMOVIC efforts vis-à-vis Iraq makes it painfully clear that such transparency was lacking in Iraq and that most Iraqi defectors and intelligence sources outside Iraq manufactured information, circulated unsubstantiated information, or simply lied. Breakthroughs do occur, but HUMINT is normally inadequate, untrustworthy, or a failure; and these shortcomings cannot usually be corrected with data based on other kinds of intelligence. Either inside information is available or it is not. When it is, imagery and signals intelligence can do more to indicate that HUMINT is wrong or suspect than it can do to reveal the truth.

Even leaders of a proliferating country may not have an accurate picture of the success of their efforts, and they most probably do not have a clear picture of the accuracy, lethality, reliability, and effects of their weapons. U.S. and British research efforts have long shown that even sophisticated technical models of the performance and lethality of chemical, biological, and nuclear weapons and their delivery systems can be grossly wrong, or require massive levels of human testing that are impractical even for closed authoritarian societies. No declassified intelligence report on any proliferation effort in any developing country has yet indicated that Iraq or another proliferator has sophisticated technical and testing models. Intelligence cannot collect data that do not exist.

Even if a nation's war plans and doctrine are known—which is unlikely—they may not be relevant. Many countries almost certainly acquire and deploy their weapons without developing detailed war plans or doctrines. Leaders may treat such weapons as symbols or deterrents and have only unformed plans for their actual use. Targeting and escalatory doctrine may be nominal or highly unrealistic. An actual crisis could then lead to a completely different approach to using such weapons, depending on the enemy's behavior. The resulting "escalation ladder" may bear no relation to the peacetime intentions of either side, nor to any game or model of efficient deterrence and use. Moreover, the inability on both sides to target and predict the weapons' effects—and simultaneously manage conventional and WMD combat—can result in highly random combat.

Problems of Intelligence Collection

The long series of UNSCOM, UNMOVIC, and IAEA reports shows that proliferating nations like Iraq are well aware of problems of intelligence collection and they know how to exploit them.

Iraq and other developing powers that are sophisticated enough to proliferate are also sophisticated enough to have a good understanding of many of the strengths and limitations of modern intelligence sensors, the timing and duration of satellite coverage, and the methods used to track imports and technology transfer. They have learned to cover and conceal, deceive, and create smaller and better-disseminated activities.

Intelligence collection on proliferation relies on finding key imports and technology transfers, but such data usually only cover a small fraction of the actual effort on the part of the proliferating country, and the information collected is often vague and uncertain, in part because importers and smugglers have every incentive to lie and are familiar with ways to defeat intelligence collection and import controls. When information does become available, it is often impossible to put in context, and a given import or technology transfer can often be used in many ways other than proliferation. Available import data can hint at the character of a proliferation effort but give no reliable picture of the overall activity.

Even when data are available on specific imports or technology transfers, the data often present three serious problems:

- The destination of the import or transfer is unknown;
- The use of the import is also unknown, as is how it is integrated into the overall effort—whether it is integrated into ongoing R&D or weapons production, procured or stockpiled for later use, or is the result of an experiment or a mistake that is never further exploited; and
- Many imports have civilian uses or other military uses, and so-called dual-use imports may have legitimate uses.

In most cases, the countries that are proliferating and clandestinely importing technology can import what they need or develop it internally. Creating effective and well-managed programs in these countries has often proved to be difficult or almost impossible, however, as has integrating complex mixes of technology into effective systems. Also, in many countries, managers or heads of such programs lack the experience to analyze with objectivity their own efforts, or they deliberately lie to their political superiors. Few physical indicators allow intelligence assessment of the effectiveness of a clandestine program's management or of the level of systems integration. The absence of any clear evidence and indicators encourages worst-case analysis.

Reliable benchmarks and measures of effectiveness are few. Even transparent access to a nation's efforts to proliferate would often lead to important uncertainties about the lethality and quality of its CBRN weapons activities and its missile and other delivery programs. For example, the level of quality control in the production of key weapons components can be so uncertain that it is impossible to determine weapons' workability. There may be too few tests to establish reliability, and a country may rely on engineering and simulation methods that simply cannot be accurately assessed. It is almost axiomatic that intelligence cannot collect what the proliferator does not know. And transparency is nonexistent for nuclear weapons design, the quality of biological agent development and production, the quality of chemical agent development and production, and missile reliability. Collection on these topics requires a level of access that is not credible.

Technical parameters for measuring weapons effectiveness are sometimes unreliable. Both the weapons development and arms control communities often take for granted technical measures that may have little or no real-world meaning. Collection is based on the assumption that the proliferator knows its level of effectiveness or that measures and standards used by developed countries for assessing Western programs also apply to developing countries. The result often blurs the distinction between collection and analysis, and creates several problems.

Nuclear weapons design and effectiveness. No proliferating country has conducted an adequate set of weapons tests to characterize fully its weapons or, in most cases, allow that country to predict the reliability and yield of its weapons. India and Pakistan have claimed far higher yields than they have been able to test, and they have lied about the yields of the weapons they have tested. Other countries—Israel, for example—absent any known test data are credited with thermonuclear or boosted weapons designs of very high efficiency (and low weight). The level of other countries' fissile enrichment is often assumed to meet U.S. weapons-grade standards, although material with less than one-third of such enrichment could produce a fissile event. The triggering and high-explosive lens design are assumed to have a given level of quality. In short, practically all aspects of a weapons design and assessments of its effectiveness may have to be based on country claims or mirror imaging.

Biological weapons design and effectiveness.   Studies by the U.S. Army and others indicate that the level of uncertainty surrounding estimates of the lethality of a nuclear weapon can reach two orders of magnitude because of the inability to know how well a given agent is produced and weaponized and because inherent uncertainties surround the use of weapons that have never had large-scale human testing and whose behavior will not mimic natural outbreaks. These problems are compounded by the fact that the method of delivering wet or dry agents makes a major impact on lethality; often the strain of disease being used is unknown, and no empirical data are available for estimating the lethality of mixes (or cocktails) of different biological agents delivered at or near the same time. The proliferators themselves probably have no realistic basis for estimating the real-world lethality of the weapons being developed or deployed.

Suspect models and lethality data are used for determining the threat posed by infectious diseases, usually based on natural outbreaks that may have little relation to military or terrorist use. The nominal data used for such estimates usually are not based on statistically relevant historical data for infectivity and lethality, and they tend to use point estimates rather than a range based on the classical statistical definition of sigma. The assumption is made that the disease strain is known or behaves according to prediction. These problems are compounded because the proliferators rarely have a realistic basis from which to estimate the real-world lethality of the weapons.

Chemical weapons design and effectiveness.   Although chemical weapons are less lethal than biological and nuclear weapons, they present many of the same problems. Without testing or empirical experience, lethality estimates are speculative at best, a problem compounded by countries' ability to handle the complex targeting and meteorological data necessary to achieve high lethality as well as the sheer randomness of many real-world delivery conditions. Again, the proliferators probably do not possess a realistic basis for estimating their weapons' real-world lethality.

Radiological weapons.   The development of crude contaminates is relatively easy, but the technology for distributing lethal material over a wide area is highly complex and theoretical. Most devices will produce alpha and beta effects with limited lethality and decontamination problems. If such weapons are improvised, however, the attacker may use almost any agent at hand, and the result could be far more lethal. Radiological weapons therefore tend to be highly random, and intelligence collection may be impossible.

Missile/aircraft/UAV-range payload. The range of a given delivery device is often estimated with a theoretical calculation that is based on a nominal payload of, for example, 1,000 kilograms (and with assumed aerodynamic efficiency). The real-world device may be much heavier or lighter, and it is usually impossible to know what proportion makes up the weapon compared with other components. A country may never test a real weapon to maximum range or fly such sorties. As a result, range estimates may have little real-world validity.

Accuracy vs. reliability vs. targeting. Both the proliferators and intelligence analysts assume for their estimates that the weapons actually work as they were designed, are accurately targeted, and are delivered so that they detonate to achieve the desired effect. The chances of most developing countries accomplishing this consistently—if ever—are negligible; however, there is no clear way to assess the impact of random error.

Misuse of CEP. Many estimates attempt to apply circular error probable (CEP) to collection and assessment. In practice, CEP assumes sufficient data exist to estimate where 50 percent of the weapons go if the entire delivery system and guidance function perfectly. CEP then describes the length of the radius from the aim point. Quite aside from the fact that most developing countries do not test enough to produce empirical CEPs, this measure ignores that half the weapons will go somewhere else in a far more random pattern along the weapon's vector and that reliability and targeting can critically degrade actual performance.

Warhead/bomb/device design. The actual weapon or agent is only part of assessing proliferation; the physical nature of a warhead or a bomb can be equally critical. For example, the timing of height of burst and efficiency of dissemination may be more important in terms of real-world lethality than the chemical or biological agent used, and will be critical in determining the level of fallout and the trade-offs between radiation-thermal-blast in a nuclear weapon. Reentry effects can have a major impact as can sprayer design.

Production capacity vs. actual capability. Analysts use the theoretical or nominal design production capacity because no data are available on actual capability.

Force strength. Deployed forces are active forces, and nominal strength is actual strength. Although few developing countries come close to achieving high readiness rates, or ever supply all of their combat units with complete unit equipment (UE) or table of organization and equipment (TO&E), analysts assume they are combat ready and have the required or nominal number of launchers, delivery vehicles, and weapons.

Psychological effects. Psychological effects are theoretical or unknown. Nations and terrorists both may use weapons for demonstrative or psychological effect, but the impact is largely speculative.

Problems of Intelligence Analysis

Many difficulties that arise in the analysis of the WMD capabilities of Iraq and other countries are the result of earlier problems in collection. Details of U.S., British, and allied intelligence analyses remain classified, but background discussions with intelligence analysts and users reveal additional problems in analyzing the WMD threat:

Collection uncertainties. Uncertainties surrounding information collection on virtually all proliferation and WMD programs are so great that it is impossible to produce meaningful point estimates. As the CIA has shown in some of its past public estimates of missile proliferation, the intelligence community must first develop a matrix of what is and is not known about a given aspect of proliferation in a given country, and it must include careful footnotes or qualification of the problems in each key source. It must then deal with uncertainty by creating estimates that show a range of possible current and projected capabilities and carefully qualify each case. At least three scenarios or cases need to be analyzed for each major aspect of proliferation in each country—something approaching a best, a most likely, and a worst case.

Compartmentation. Even under these conditions, the resulting analytic effort faces serious problems. Security compartmentation within each major aspect of collection and analysis severely limits the flow of data to working analysts. Expansion of analytic staffs has sharply increased the barriers to the flow of data and has brought on a large number of junior analysts who can do little more than update past analyses and judgments. Far too little analysis is subjected to technical review by those who have actually worked on weapons development; and typical analyses of delivery programs, warheads and weapons, and chemical, biological, and nuclear proliferation is compartmented. Instead of a free flow of data and exchange of analytic conclusions— fusion of intelligence—analysis is stovepiped into separate areas. The larger the staffs become, the more the stovepiping occurs.

Exaggeration. Analysis usually focuses on technical capability and not on the problems of management and systems integration that often limit proliferation in the real world. Analysis is thus pushed toward exaggerating the probable level of proliferation, particularly because technical capability is often assumed if collection cannot provide all the necessary information.

Faulty assumptions. Where data are available on past holdings of weapons and the capability to produce such weapons—such as data on chemical weapons feedstocks and biological growth material—the intelligence effort usually produces estimates of the maximum size of the possible current holding of weapons and WMD materials. Although ranges are often shown and estimates are usually qualified with uncertainty, typical consumers of the intelligence focus on the worst case in terms of actual current capability. For Iraq, this was compounded by approximately 12 years of lies and a disbelief that a dictatorship obsessed with record keeping would not possess records if it had destroyed weapons and materials. The resulting UNSCOM, UNMOVIC, and IAEA reports thus assumed that there was a substantial risk that little or no destruction had occurred.

Orientation of analysis. Intelligence analysis has long been oriented more toward arms control and counterproliferation than to war fighting, although the Defense Intelligence Agency and the military services have attempted to shift the focus of analysis. The situation is very different when it comes to dealing with war-fighting choices, particularly issues like preemption and targeting. Assumptions of capability can lead to unnecessary preemption, overtargeting, inability to prioritize, and a failure to create the detailed collection and analysis necessary to support war fighters down to the battalion level. Field commanders are often forced to rely on field teams with limited capability and expertise and to overreact to any potential threat or warning indicator.

Outside experts. The intelligence community does bring outside experts into the process, but the experts often advise in general terms rather than participate in a cleared review of the intelligence product, which leads to a less helpful result. The use of personnel with security clearances in U.S. laboratories and with other areas of expertise is inadequate and often presents major problems because those consulted are not brought fully into the analysis of intelligence and provided all necessary data.

Alternative analyses. The intelligence community tries to avoid explicit statements of its shortcomings in collection and methods, and it repeats past agreed judgments on a lowest-common-denominator level, particularly in intelligence products that circulate to many consumers. Attempts at independent outside analysis—B teams—are not subject to the review and controls enforced on intelligence analysis, however; and the teams, collection data, and methods of the B teams are often selected to prove specific points rather than provide an objective counterpoint to finished analysis.

Bureaucratic failings. Time limitations, bureaucratic momentum, and poor supervision lead to failures of both review and zero-based analysis. Reviews of unclassified reports show endless repetition of prior assessments and conclusions without updated content review and without a comprehensive review of past judgments.

Pressures from Consumers of Intelligence

Policymakers and users create pressures that impede accurate reporting on uncertainty. In many cases intelligence cannot resolve the problems and shortcomings in the above list, and it will be critical that both the intelligence community and consumers frankly admit the level of uncertainty involved—a difficult challenge. The users of intelligence are in the best of times intolerant of analysis that consists of a wide range of qualifications and uncertainties, and the best of times does not exist when urgent policy and war-fighting decisions need to be made. Either typical users force the intelligence process to reach something approaching a definitive set of conclusions, or they estimate the conclusions themselves.

Intelligence analysts and managers are all too aware of consumer demands. Experience has taught them that complex analyses—with their alternative cases, probability estimates, and qualifications about uncertainty—generally go unused or make policymakers and commanders impatient with the entire intelligence process. In the real world, hard choices result in estimates that can actually be used and acted upon, and these choices must be made by either the intelligence community or the user.

CHAPTER EIGHT

BEYOND IRAQ

The United States must look beyond Iraq—its first current war—and deal with its other security interests and wars. No strategy that focuses on Iraq alone is an adequate approach to the future. Almost without sensing the drift, the United States has found itself enmeshed in four separate but simultaneous conflicts. The most obvious war is Iraq, but each of the other conflicts also requires at least some shifts in U.S. policy.

AFGHANISTAN

Afghanistan has become the not-quite-forgotten war. Americans and America's allies die there, but not as regularly as in Iraq. Nation building is in crisis in Afghanistan but at less cost and largely without high-profile media examination.

Victory, however, has proved to be as relative in Afghanistan—its second current war—as in Iraq. The Taliban has mutated and is again fighting; Al Qaeda has lost many of its leaders but also has mutated and relocated some operations to Pakistan; internal tensions in Afghanistan threaten to make its central government the government of only a Kabulstan; and the spillover of Islamic extremism into Central and South Asia continues.

Moreover, the United States (and a number of its allies) are repeating many of the nation-building mistakes of Iraq in a country with far fewer resources and far less hope. The security effort is marginal and carried out on the cheap, and each incremental security fix lags behind the growth of the problem.

The creation of a political Kabulstan is confused with the creation of a true Afghan government, and economic aid efforts seem to be in perpetual denial about the fact the country has no near-term basis for an economy other than poppy growing and illegal drug production. Basic lessons about the need for objective planning and adequate resources are ignored. Afghanistan remains a real war, and the United States cannot pay for its victory in Iraq by leaving Afghanistan without the military capabilities to pursue the Taliban and Al Qaeda.

Aspects of the task in Afghanistan may be easier than in Iraq, but only if the United States is willing to pay for Afghan and allied nation building and military forces that can secure the country. The North Atlantic Treaty Organization (NATO) is already in Afghanistan. Germany has already played a critical role. Reducing U.S. global strategic overstretch could be achieved through the pursuit of an allied strategy in Afghanistan, which would free as many U.S. resources as possible for Iraq.

The United States cannot deal with the Afghan conflict by simply transferring the country's security to NATO or international control. If it tries, the almost certain results would be a resurgence of the Taliban or another form of Islamic extremism, continued warlordism, and a drug-based economy—with an inevitable spillover into the Middle East and Central Asia. The effort need not be on the scale of the U.S. effort in Iraq, but the United States must provide substantial resources for a period of five to ten more years, at a cost of $5 to $10 billion more in aid than it has currently budgeted.

WAR ON TERRORISM

The broader war on terrorism continues, but this third war often generates more heat than light. The Bush administration sometimes focuses on Iraq, believing that Americans (and presumably the world) will accept the war after the war there if it can be blamed on terrorism and Al Qaeda—a better alternative than the perception of administration failure to prepare for conflict termination and nation building.

The faults are solidly bipartisan. Rather than focusing on specific terrorist movements hostile to the United States and its allies, many in the U.S. Congress and media have used rhetoric to make the war on terrorism seem like a war on Islam and the Arab world. Others continue trying to make Saudi Arabia the focus, even though the Saudis are fighting their own battle against Al Qaeda.

The reality is that the war on terrorism is against hostile Islamic extremist movements and cells the world over; it is a global conflict and exists not only in Iraq, Saudi Arabia, and Afghanistan. The primary fighting is within Islamic states, between secular leaders and religious extremists—Shi`a, Salafi, Sufi, and neo-Wahhabi. It is this secular–religious extremist clash within a civilization that spills over into other regions, and the terrorists and extremists often use the United States as a proxy target for their efforts to change or overthrow local regimes.

The United States faces enduring threats from terrorism and violent Islamic extremism, driven by all of the midterm and long-term forces discussed earlier. The United States cannot afford to deal with Islam and the Arab world in terms of ideological prejudice, whether neoconservatism or neoliberalism. The United States needs to look to pragmatism, neorealism, and a return to the internationalism that has shaped its most successful national security policies since World War II.

The United States on its own cannot afford to engage every terrorist movement, and it risks alienating and radicalizing peoples and movements throughout the Islamic world if it does. It needs to create local partnerships with key nations like Saudi Arabia and Indonesia. It needs to focus systematically on the differences among the various Sufi, Salafi, neo-Wahhabi, and Shi`a movements, and address each separately on terms best tailored to defeating each group's violence and extremism.

The U.S. government needs to make a far more visible effort to clarify its understanding of these nuances and of the fact that it is fighting a relatively small minority of extremists and not the Arab world or all of Islam. In the process, the United States must also clarify that it is seeking to persuade other countries of the worth of its values and is not seeking to impose its values without their consent.

The United States should once again start thinking in terms of decades. It must make a long-term effort to work with the nations of the Arab and Islamic worlds to both fight terrorist movements and encourage the full range of well-defined evolutionary reforms best suited to each given country at a given time.

The United States cannot succeed if it continues call vaguely for democracy rather than labor industriously in well-planned, nation-by-nation efforts to achieve evolutionary reform. In fact, the current U.S. approach threatens to turn the word "democracy" into a vulgarism, a synonym for half-reasoned U.S. efforts to force its own political system on other countries or simply serve its own interests through regime change. President Bush did advance support for a more nuanced approach in his speech on democracy in the Middle East in early November 2003; however, U.S. neoconservatives and neoliberals often preoccupy themselves with slogans in a world where the net result of what they recommend would often be "one man, one vote, one time."

Elections are only one part of what should be a carefully tailored country-by-country effort to achieve evolutionary change and reform. The first step is often to improve human rights and the quality of the rule of law. Concurrent assistance with achieving economic reform and facing demographic problems should have equal priority. Consultative institutions, realization of the responsibilities and benefits of voting, political parties based on people, media that support honest elective processes, and transparency of resource use and government management can all be preconditions for effective pluralism.

The United States must look beyond the word "democracy" and remember that it is not democracy but instead a republic, with three branches of government, a bill of rights, and certain limits on majority rule. It has a government that protects the individual over the majority and preserves the rights of all through the constitutional and legal limitations on the power of the federal government and checks and balances within government. It is revolution, not evolution, that brings misery to nations where it occurs, and it is revolution that brings violence and hostility to the United States. It is evolution that the United States should encourage.

ARAB-ISRAELI CONFLICT

The fourth war does not involve direct use of U.S. troops, but the Arab people and the Islamic world perceive the United States as a cobelligerent with Israel. The Israeli-Palestinian conflict involves the United States strategically almost as deeply as if it were a belligerent. The United States is Israel's ally and its main source of aid and military equipment, and the Islamic world and most of the Arabs conclude that the United States is partly responsible for Israel's actions.

A struggle the United States and Israel perceive as a struggle against terrorism and extremism is perceived by Arabs and Iran as a struggle against Palestinians, who in turn are struggling for liberation and independence. Far too often, Arab media are anything but objective.

Worse, the U.S. presence in Iraq is increasingly perceived among Arabs as a replica of the Israeli occupation in Gaza and the West Bank. A flood of conspiracy theories charges that the United States is copying Israeli tactics and that U.S. actions in Iraq are dictated by Israel.

The United States does not have good options. It cannot abandon Israel or sacrifice its security, but now it must deal with two failed leaderships and two peoples who do not possess faith in each other or the capability of seeing the world through the other's eyes. The United States will be at a major disadvantage in Iraq, in the war on terrorism, and in the Arab and Islamic worlds as long as the Israeli-Palestinian war continues.

The United States should plan for the Israeli-Palestinian War to be a major strategic liability for the next five to ten years. The United States can do nothing to prevent Arab and Islamic media from reporting one-sided images of the conflict and blaming the United States in part for Israel's actions. Yet the United States cannot abandon Israel and may well confront the fact that Israel's deteriorating economy will require additional aid.

There is no way out of this dilemma other than a continuing, high-visibility U.S. effort to create a peace, regardless of how many times new initiatives fail. The peace process will not win Arab hearts and minds, but it can increase Arab tolerance. Moreover, even more than U.S. interests, Israel's ultimate strategic interests lie in a successful peace. Israel cannot sustain its social structure and economy through constant, low-level war. The United States will never be at existential risk because of Middle Eastern proliferation; in a matter of years, Israel could be.

The broad course of action the United States has laid out in the road map is the correct one, but the timing may well be a matter of a decade, and the United States cannot either achieve its goals or serve the true strategic interests of the Israeli people by simply supporting the Israeli government of the day. Intolerance of terrorism should be accompanied by an equal intolerance of settlements and separation.

The security situation will be demanding during continued war and any peace. The United States must support Israel in fighting terrorism, and it should support Israel in pushing the Palestinians into a real effort to suppress terrorist movements. But this does not mean supporting Israel's Sharon government and its impossible standards for Palestinian behavior. The United States must also resist every Israeli and pro-Israeli effort to drag it into confrontations with Syria, Hizballah, Hamas, and the Palestinian Islamic Jihad unless it is possible to prove that these entities target the United States. Israel's problems and priorities are Israel's, not America's. The United States cannot afford to wander off in search of enemies.

The United States must exercise extreme caution about any plans to put U.S. forces on the ground to separate Israelis and Palestinians. U.S. troops would become a natural target for every Islamic extremist movement that seeks to broaden the scope of the war on terrorism and every media outlet that delights in broadcasting images of retaliation against Palestinians.

The United States needs to think hard about what an international military presence in Israel really means and work with its allies toward options that both Israelis and Palestinians can accept. Massive new aid—to a new Palestinian state and to Jordan to ensure the success of any peace process—will be needed over a decade to provide the necessary tools of nation building.

CONFLICTS IN WAITING

Other potential struggles are waiting in the wings although it is far from clear that war will actually occur. These flashpoints include Iran and Iranian acquisition of nuclear weapons, North Korea's efforts to proliferate and its constant stream of threats, and the much lower level of tension across the Taiwan Strait. At a less intense level, because the United States is also involved in a war on drugs in Colombia, some degree of involvement in Colombia's civil war is inevitable.

CHAPTER NINE

REALITY AND CHOICES

The image of a quick and decisive victory is almost always an illusion, but it is the image many Americans want and expect. One thousand or more dead in Iraq is not Vietnam, but they are deaths that must be justified, explained, and explained honestly—not with ephemeral slogans. The rising defense budget and supplements of the past few years are also likely to be the rule and not the exception. The United States may well have to spend another percent or more of its GNP on sustained combat and international intervention overseas although no U.S. politician is yet willing to admit this.

America faces hard political choices, and facing them will take exceptional leadership and courage in both the election year of 2004 and for decades to come. The choices require bipartisanship of a kind that has faded since the Cold War, and neither neoconservative nor neoliberal ideology has been helpful. America's public policy institutions, think tanks, and media must move beyond sound bites and simple solutions, as America's politicians and military planners also must. 2004 will be a very tough year, and it will be part of a very tough decade.

ABOUT THE AUTHOR

Anthony H. Cordesman holds the Arleigh A. Burke Chair in Strategy at CSIS. He is also a military analyst for ABC News and a frequent commentator on National Public Radio and the BBC. His television commentary has been featured prominently during the Iraq War, the Gulf War, Desert Fox, the conflict in Kosovo, and the fighting in Afghanistan.

Cordesman is the author of a wide range of studies on U.S. security policy, energy policy, and Middle East policy. He has served as national security assistant to Senator John McCain of the Senate Armed Services Committee, as director of intelligence assessment in the Office of the Secretary of Defense, as civilian assistant to the deputy secretary of defense, and as director of policy and planning for resource applications in the Department of Energy. He has also served in a number of other government positions, including in the State Department and on NATO International Staff, and he has had numerous foreign assignments, including posts in Lebanon, Egypt, and Iran, with extensive work in Saudi Arabia and the Gulf.

Cordesman is the author of more than 20 books, including most recently *The Iraq War: Strategy, Tactics, and Military Lessons* (CSIS, 2003), *Saudi Arabia Enters the Twenty-first Century: The Military and National Security Dimensions* (Praeger/CSIS, 2003), *Saudi Arabia Enters the Twenty-first Century: The Political, Foreign Policy, Economic, and Energy Dimensions* (Praeger/CSIS, 2003), *The Lessons of Afghanistan: War Fighting, Intelligence, and Force Transformation* (CSIS, 2002), *Terrorism, Asymmetric Warfare, and Weapons of Mass Destruction* (Praeger/CSIS, 2002), *Cyber-threats, Information Warfare, and Critical Infrastructure Protection* (Praeger/CSIS, 2002), and *Strategic Threats and National Missile Defenses* (Praeger/CSIS, 2002).